Remote Teaching and Learning in the Middle and High ELA Classroom

Teaching in remote, distance, and hybrid environments can be overwhelming and confusing and poses many challenges for novice and veteran teachers alike. This book guides teachers through the best practices of English language arts (ELA) instruction and helps them reflect on ways to apply those practices in remote learning and envision future instruction that draws from the most useful aspects of educational innovations. Understanding that remote teaching looks different in each subject, Ruday and Cassidy identify methods specifically designed for middle and high school ELA classrooms.

Designed for use in remote, hybrid, and hyflex environments with synchronous or asynchronous learning, this resource gives teachers a toolbox of research-backed recommendations, ideas, examples, and practices for teaching in unpredictable and new environments. Ruday and Cassidy address essential topics, including writing, grammar, and reading instruction; assessment; differentiation; culturally relevant teaching; family engagement and communication; technology; professional self-care; and more. Teachers will come away with ready-to-implement strategies and insights for high-quality instruction that can be adapted to any kind of remote learning environment.

Sean Ruday is Associate Professor of English education at Longwood University and a former classroom teacher. He frequently writes and presents on innovative ways to improve students' literacy learning. You can follow him on Twitter @SeanRuday and visit his website at www.seanruday.weebly.com.

Jennifer Cassidy is an eighth-grade English teacher and English department chair for Chesapeake Public Schools, Virginia. You can follow her on Twitter @Jenn_Cassidy_.

Other Eye on Education Books Available from Routledge
(www.routledge.com/eyeoneducation)

Remote Teaching and Learning in the Elementary ELA Classroom
Instructional Strategies and Best Practices
Sean Ruday and Taylor M. Jacobson

The Elementary School Grammar Toolkit, Second Edition
Using Mentor Texts to Teach Standards-Based Language and Grammar in Grades 3–5
Sean Ruday

The Middle School Grammar Toolkit, Second Edition
Using Mentor Texts to Teach Standards-Based Language and Grammar in Grades 6–8
Sean Ruday

Inquiry-Based Literature Instruction in the 6–12 Classroom
A Hands-on Guide for Deeper Learning
Sean Ruday and Katie Caprino

The Multimedia Writing Toolkit
Helping Students Incorporate Graphics and Videos for Authentic Purposes, Grades 3–8
Sean Ruday

The Informational Writing Toolkit
Using Mentor Texts in Grades 3–5
Sean Ruday

The Argument Writing Toolkit
Using Mentor Texts in Grades 6–8
Sean Ruday

The Narrative Writing Toolkit
Using Mentor Texts in Grades 3–8
Sean Ruday

The First-Year English Teacher's Guidebook
Strategies for Success
Sean Ruday

Culturally Relevant Teaching in the English Language Arts Classroom
Sean Ruday

Rigor in the Remote Learning Classroom
Instructional Tips and Strategies
Barbara R. Blackburn

Remote Teaching and Learning in the Middle and High ELA Classroom

Instructional Strategies and Best Practices

Sean Ruday and Jennifer Cassidy

Taylor & Francis Group

NEW YORK AND LONDON

First published 2022
by Routledge
605 Third Avenue, New York, NY 10158

and by Routledge
2 Park Square, Milton Park, Abingdon, Oxon, OX14 4RN

Routledge is an imprint of the Taylor & Francis Group, an informa business

© 2022 Sean Ruday and Jennifer Cassidy

The right of Sean Ruday and Jennifer Cassidy to be identified as authors of this work has been asserted by them in accordance with sections 77 and 78 of the Copyright, Designs and Patents Act 1988.

All rights reserved. The purchase of this copyright material confers the right on the purchasing institution to photocopy or download pages which bear the support material icon and a copyright line at the bottom of the page. No other parts of this book may be reprinted or reproduced or utilised in any form or by any electronic, mechanical, or other means, now known or hereafter invented, including photocopying and recording, or in any information storage or retrieval system, without permission in writing from the publishers.

Trademark notice: Product or corporate names may be trademarks or registered trademarks, and are used only for identification and explanation without intent to infringe.

Library of Congress Cataloging-in-Publication Data
Names: Ruday, Sean, author. | Cassidy, Jennifer, author.
Title: Remote teaching and learning in the middle and high ELA classroom : instructional strategies and best practices / Sean Ruday and Jennifer Cassidy.
Identifiers: LCCN 2021018898 (print) | LCCN 2021018899 (ebook) | ISBN 9780367741624 (hardback) | ISBN 9780367723965 (paperback) | ISBN 9781003156338 (ebook)
Subjects: LCSH: Distance education. | English language—Study and teaching (Middle school) | English language—Study and teaching (High school) | Web-based instruction. | Blended learning. | Technological innovations.
Classification: LCC LC5800 .R82 2022 (print) | LCC LC5800 (ebook) | DDC 371.35—dc23
LC record available at https://lccn.loc.gov/2021018898
LC ebook record available at https://lccn.loc.gov/2021018899

ISBN: 978-0-367-74162-4 (hbk)
ISBN: 978-0-367-72396-5 (pbk)
ISBN: 978-1-003-15633-8 (ebk)

Typeset in Palatino
by Apex CoVantage, LLC

Access the Support Material: www.routledge.com/9780367723965

Contents

Meet the Authors	vii
Acknowledgments	viii
Support Material	ix
Introduction: Visions and Decisions in a New Educational Environment	1

Section I: The New "Classroom" — 9

1 Building a Learning Community in the Time of Remote Instruction	11
2 Class Discussion and Student Collaboration in a New Era	20

Section II: The Potential of Remote ELA Instruction — 31

3 A New Format of Writing and Grammar Instruction	33
4 Literature Instruction in the Remote Environment	47
5 Culturally Relevant and Sustaining Teaching and Learning in Remote Contexts	61
6 The Role of Inquiry in Remote Teaching and Learning	73
7 Assessing Student Learning	84

Section III: Teacher Roles in a New World — 99

8 Strategies for Communication With Students and Caregivers	101
9 Reflecting on Technology	107
10 Taking Care of Yourself	112

Section IV: Resources — 117

11 Key Takeaway Ideas — 119

References — 125

Section V: Appendices — 129

Appendix A Forms, Templates, and Graphic Organizers — 131

Appendix B A Guide for Book Studies — 135

Meet the Authors

Sean Ruday is Associate Professor and Program Coordinator of English Education at Longwood University and a former classroom teacher. He began his teaching career at a public school in Brooklyn, New York, and has taught English and language arts at public and private schools in New York, Massachusetts, and Virginia. He holds a BA from Boston College, an MA from New York University, and a PhD from the University of Virginia. Some publications in which his works have appeared are *Issues in Teacher Education*, the *Journal of Teaching Writing*, the *Journal of Language and Literacy Education*, and *Contemporary Issues in Technology and Teacher Education*. Sean frequently writes and presents on innovative ways to improve students' literacy learning. You can follow Sean on Twitter at @SeanRuday and visit his website at *www.seanruday.weebly.com*.

Jennifer Cassidy is a second-year teacher working for Chesapeake Public Schools. She teaches eighth-grade English and serves as her school's English department chair. Jenn is a graduate of Longwood University and studied under Dr. Sean Ruday. She is a native of Chesapeake and currently resides in Norfolk, Virginia. Keep up with Jenn on Twitter @Jenn_Cassidy_.

Acknowledgments

Sean's Acknowledgments

I want to thank everyone at Routledge Eye on Education—especially amazing editor Karen Adler—for the insight, guidance, and support.

I would like to thank my parents, Bob and Joyce Ruday. I am grateful for their encouragement in all aspects of my life.

Finally, I want to thank my wife, Clare Ruday. I can't imagine my life without the happiness she brings to it.

Jenn's Acknowledgments

Thank you, Routledge Eye on Education, for this incredible opportunity.

Dr. Ruday, it is always a pleasure to learn from and work with you. Thank you for believing in me and offering encouragement along the way.

A special thank you goes to my family for their unwavering support. Thank you to my biggest cheerleaders: Mom, Dad, Grandma Clare, and Michael. Your support and love mean the world.

Support Material

Many of the tools discussed and displayed in this book are also available on the Routledge website as Adobe Acrobat files. Permission has been granted to purchasers of this book to download these tools and print them. You can access these downloads by visiting www.routledge.com/9780367723965. Then click on the tab that says "Support Material" and select the files. They will begin downloading to your computer.

Introduction

Visions and Decisions in a New Educational Environment

For us, the new educational environment of remote and distance learning has led to a great deal of reflection—and, since you're reading this book, we suspect it may have done the same for you. As we've thought about our work with our students (Jennifer with her middle schoolers and Sean with the preservice teachers he mentors and the middle and high school classes with which he works), we've considered what English language arts instruction should look like in the many forms of remote and distance learning. We've asked ourselves questions such as the following:

- How can remote English language arts instruction incorporate research-based best instructional practices?
- How can it foster meaningful class discussions and student collaboration?
- How can we as teachers work for equitable educational opportunities for our students in the remote learning context?
- How can we incorporate culturally relevant and sustaining instructional practices in remote English language arts instruction?
- What are some especially important ideas to consider regarding the many instructional technological resources being promoted?
- What are the best ways for teachers to communicate with students and their caregivers?
- How can teachers be sure to take care of themselves in this new and challenging time?

These questions, and others like them, form the fundamental basis of this book, which we've designed to provide middle and high school English language arts teachers with a practical and comprehensive resource that describes how to implement the best practices of English language arts instruction in today's world of remote instruction and beyond. We say "beyond" because the ideas and strategies discussed in this book are not only relevant during the time schools have moved online due to COVID-19 but also in the future when administrators, teachers, and students can think about what instructional practices incorporated during this time may be useful to further enhance English language arts instruction.

We decided to write this book to provide teachers with a thorough, research-based, and practice-ready book that conveys clear ideas about effective English language arts instruction and describes specific ways to put those ideas into action in the various distance learning settings in which today's educators find themselves while also giving them the tools and insights to think about ways they might continue to utilize some of these practices. As the authors of this book, we have two main complementary goals. The first is to help teachers think about and identify the best methods of English language arts instruction in the middle and high school settings, such as culturally relevant teaching, inquiry-based learning, mentor text use, and student collaboration. The second is to provide teachers with concrete recommendations, ideas, and examples to help them put these best-practice strategies into action in their remote teaching practice. Since there are a variety of ways that educational practices in today's world can look, such as completely online, hybrid learning, and hyflex constructions, we discuss how the book's instructional insights can be adapted for this range of formats. We want teachers to finish reading this book and think, "I know about high-quality English language arts instruction, *and* I know how to implement it in remote learning!"

Effective Remote English Language Arts Instruction

It's so easy for teachers to be overwhelmed with all the technological tools, apps, and programs often brought up in conversations about remote learning. Because of these many options and innovations, teachers may feel anxious due to a lack of familiarity with some programs and feel pressured to utilize them without understanding what they are. While many technological tools can positively impact teaching and learning, we encourage teachers to think carefully about these resources and reflect on their potential usefulness before utilizing them in remote instruction. An especially effective way to do this is to consider whether specific technological tools, resources, and programs align with their pedagogical goals and are effective ways of achieving those goals (Ruday, 2016; Young & Bush, 2004). Instead of starting with a resource, app, or program and making instruction align with its features, we encourage teachers to decide on their instructional objectives and then select tools that are the best ways to fit that objective.

We believe that the best remote English language arts instruction is not rooted in a specific app, program, or website but is rooted instead in thoughtful decision-making that carefully considers the relevant learning goals and student needs and uses that information to identify the best ways to help students learn. Teachers will certainly need to consider their available resources and instructional contexts in this decision-making process, but we feel that the best remote instruction is the kind that maximizes student learning and uses available programs as vehicles for that learning. For example, if we English teachers want to hold one-on-one writing conferences with our students, we should select resources and programs that facilitate this type of interaction. Similarly, if our objective is to engage students in inquiry-based learning that gives them opportunities to create and investigate questions that matter to them, we would identify and use tools that align with this instructional practice. By being intentional with the instructional resources we use, we can engage our students in remote English language arts instruction that maximizes their learning.

We've titled this introduction "visions and decisions in a new educational environment" because of the importance we place on aligning our beliefs about effective instructions with specific practices. Whether we teach in an in-person, remote, hybrid, or hyflex model, it's essential that we make decisions about teaching and learning that correspond with our beliefs about the best practices of English language arts instruction. For instance, if one of our core beliefs about strong grammar instruction is that grammatical concepts are taught in the context of effective writing using mentor texts, we can make instructional decisions that put this idea into action in ways that align with the instructional modality we're using. If we believe that it's essential for students to be able to collaborate on assignments so they can share and learn from their peers' ideas, let's ensure that our instructional practices and decisions correspond with that vision.

While schools were forced into remote learning in 2020 due to the COVID-19 pandemic, it's important to note that the educational practices utilized during this time can continue to be relevant and useful even when schools return to fully in-person instruction. If some of the instructional practices utilized during remote and distance learning prove to be the best ways for us English language arts teachers to help students engage with the curriculum, we should continue to implement those practices in some form.

For example, if a tool a teacher utilizes during remote learning facilitates meaningful and effective student collaboration, that teacher can certainly look for ways to continue to make use of that tool in the future, regardless of whether the instruction is delivered remotely or not. Similarly, if a teacher finds that some remote learning components lend themselves to culturally relevant teaching, they can continue to utilize those practices and components in the future because they align with that teacher's instructional beliefs and maximize students' abilities to engage with the curriculum. Now that we've shared key aspects of our beliefs about effective English language arts instruction, let's look at what's in store in this book.

What to Expect in This Book

This book is divided into four sections that we believe work together to provide teachers with the information they need to implement high-quality English language arts instruction in a remote context. Section I, "The New 'Classroom,'" contains two chapters that address important ideas for teachers to consider as they create interactive, cohesive, and effective learning environments. Chapter 1, "Building a Learning Community in the Time of Remote Instruction," provides examples and suggestions to help teachers construct cohesive communities among their students while navigating the realities of remote and distanced learning. These insights are designed to foster learning environments in which students feel comfortable and ready to engage in learning—even if they are not in the physical classroom. Chapter 2, "Class Discussion and Student Collaboration in a New Era," provides a logical extension for the ideas in Chapter 1: once students feel comfortable in their learning communities, they can collaborate and take part in interactive discussions. This chapter describes ways for teachers to facilitate meaningful discussions and to construct collaborative activities, both of which will maximize student learning and help them feel part of a cohesive learning community. After you read this section, we want you to be able to build an educational environment in which students feel comfortable and engage your students in collaboration that facilitates their learning and their sense of community.

The book's second section, titled "The Potential of Remote ELA Instruction," discusses specific instructional tactics that represent the best practices of English language arts teaching and can be effectively adapted to remote contexts. The five chapters in this section detail important components of middle and high English language arts instruction and discuss ways teachers can implement them in a variety of distance and remote learning situations.

Chapter 3, "A New Format of Writing and Grammar Instruction," discusses how the best methods of teaching writing strategies and grammatical concepts, such as mentor text use, writing conferences, and writing workshops, can be effectively utilized when students are learning remotely. Chapter 4, "Literature Instruction in the Remote Environment," provides insights into ways we as English language arts teachers can facilitate students' responses to and discussions of literature while utilizing features and attributes of remote learning.

In Chapter 5, "Culturally Relevant and Sustaining Teaching and Learning in Remote Contexts," we discuss how teachers can incorporate the principles of culturally relevant and culturally sustaining pedagogy in remote English language arts instruction, discussing key components of culturally relevant and sustaining teaching and describing ways that remote instruction can be used to facilitate this important instructional strategy. Similarly, in Chapter 6, "The Role of Inquiry in Remote Teaching and Learning," we describe ways for teachers to utilize inquiry-based English language arts instruction in the remote learning context, sharing important aspects of this instructional approach and discussing the ways it can be effectively incorporated in remote teaching and learning. This section concludes with Chapter 7, "Assessing Student Learning"; in this chapter, we describe important assessment-related ideas to guide you as you utilize effective formative and summative assessments in the context of remote English language arts instruction. The ideas and methods discussed in this section align with the book's goal of ensuring that readers understand the key components of effective English language arts instruction and the best ways to put them into practice in remote instruction.

The third section of the book, "Teacher Roles in a New World," contains three chapters designed to guide and support teachers as they navigate the unique challenges of the remote learning environment. Chapter 8, "Strategies for Communication With Students and Caregivers," addresses one such component of the new educational world, discussing tactics educators can use to most effectively communicate with our students and their caregivers when they do not have the same level of face-to-face contact they previously did. In Chapter 9, "Reflecting on Technology," we provide insights and recommendations for teachers to use to make the technology used in their remote instruction strategic and equitable. As we discuss in more depth in Chapter 9, remote learning has highlighted important issues related to instructional technology, such as the importance of aligning technological tools with specific learning goals and being mindful of issues related to technology access. This section concludes with Chapter 10, "Taking Care of Yourself," which discusses self-care ideas especially relevant to teachers navigating the professional and personal challenges associated with the demands of remote teaching. This chapter describes ways to create work–life balance and manage stress, ensuring that educators take care of themselves so they can best help their students. After reading these three chapters, educators will have additional tools at their disposal for succeeding in a changed reality.

The book concludes with Section IV, which features information and resources designed to help you put the ideas in this book into action. Chapter 11, "Key Takeaway Ideas," describes important insights and recommendations to facilitate effective remote teaching and learning experiences for you and your students. Following that, you'll find the book's Reference section, which cites important sources that you can examine to further develop your understandings of effective remote English language arts instruction. Appendix A contains forms, templates, and graphic organizers that you can use when planning your instruction; these resources are designed to help you put the ideas and concepts discussed in this book into action as easily as possible. Finally, the "Guide for Book Studies" in Appendix B identifies thought-provoking reflection questions and prompts to consider when using this book as a book-study text. We highly recommend engaging in a book study of this text with other teachers in your professional learning network; doing so can allow you to collaboratively discuss the ideas and practices the book describes and brainstorm ways to apply its ideas to your own instruction.

For consistency and ease of use, each chapter in this book that describes an educational strategy follows a similar pattern: we discuss the chapter's focal topic, explain how it aligns with remote learning, share an example from Jennifer's work as an English teacher, provide teachers with key recommendations to consider when implementing the focal topic in their own practice, and discuss how the chapter's concept can be utilized in a wide range of instructional modalities, including entirely remote instruction (in which instruction is completely virtual), hybrid instruction (in which students are physically present in the classroom some days and engage through virtual learning other days), and hyflex instruction (in which some students are physically present in the classroom and other students join at the same time virtually). As you read this book, you'll engage with many ideas about the best practices of English instruction and with clear and concrete suggestions for enacting them in the context of remote learning. While many of us entered remote learning because of COVID-19, we, as the authors of this book, see the suggestions described in this text as having relevance beyond the pandemic. We believe that the educational innovations and remote learning tactics first employed out of necessity have the potential to have lasting impacts on education by taking advantage of technological resources, innovative practices, and 21st-century communication tools. This book will guide you as you consider research-based best practices of English language arts instruction, reflect on ways to implement those practices in remote learning, and envision future instruction that draws from the most useful aspects of educational innovations. So, if you're ready to learn more about strong English language arts teaching and learning in remote contexts, keep reading!

1

The New "Classroom"

1

Building a Learning Community in the Time of Remote Instruction

In this chapter, we explore the concept of constructing a strong learning community in the time of remote instruction, which is both a significant challenge and a key aspect of instructional learning success. The information in this chapter provides important information about the features and significance of such a community and conveys useful suggestions to consider when building a strong sense of connection among students during remote instruction. First, we explore what it means to build a learning community in the time of remote instruction, highlighting attributes, challenges, and opportunities associated with constructing a strong remote learning community. We then reflect on why doing so is especially important, which we follow with an instructional snapshot section that provides an example of Jennifer's work with her middle school students. After that, we share key recommendations for teachers to consider when building strong remote learning communities with their students. Finally, we discuss how the ideas described in this chapter can be utilized in and adapted for a wide range of modalities.

What Does It Mean to Build a Learning Community in the Time of Remote Instruction?

Take a minute and think about the term *learning community* and how it relates to English language arts instruction. What comes to your mind? It might be a teacher conducting reading and writing mini-lessons with engaged students who are challenged by the content and thinking about ways to apply their newfound knowledge. It could be students working in small groups as they synthesize important ideas from class reading. Perhaps it's students and teachers talking together about how a text, essential question, or concept relates to the contemporary world. It might even be students and teachers smiling and joking together, enjoying the strong sense of community and connection in the classroom. When we (Sean and Jennifer) think about the images that *learning community* calls to mind for us, a common theme in those images is the strong relationships that exist: the individuals in the communities we picture are learning, communicating, and interacting in ways that highlight the strong relationships in that community. We love building relationships with our students and helping them feel at home, welcome, and supported in English language arts and have developed a variety of tools and tactics to help us do so.

However, the challenge facing us and other educators around the country in the age of remote learning is how we can construct a relationship-driven and supportive learning community in the time of remote instruction. In order to think about how to do this, one early step is to reflect on what the experience of community building in a remote education environment looks like. While certain aspects of learning communities will, of course, differ between instruction entirely in person and instruction delivered in remote contexts, we feel there are common components of strong learning communities that exist across learning modalities. Strong learning communities, we believe, do the following:

- Prioritize teacher-to-student and student-to-student relationship building.
- Center students' individual interests, experiences, and identities.
- Use relevance, humor, and genuine connections to create a positive environment that facilitates comfort, learning, and risk-taking.

Although some aspects of relationship building can be different in remote learning environments, we believe that it is still possible (and very important) for teachers to work with their students to construct learning communities that foster meaningful relationships and genuine connections in all learning contexts and situations. In the next section, we look in more detail at the importance of strong learning communities that value student relationships.

Why Is This Important?

Research indicates that strong student–teacher relationships can positively impact students' abilities to succeed in school in a variety of ways (Quin, 2016).

In addition, teachers can help create supportive classroom environments in which students feel safe, are encouraged to collaborate, and are comfortable taking risks (Aspen Institute, 2017). These findings speak to what many teachers and students have noticed through their experiences: strong relationships and learning communities enhance student learning. Between the two of us, we've worked with English language arts students in a variety of school settings and have routinely noticed that building community is essential to creating an educational context that facilities successful teaching and learning.

During the time we've taught in remote contexts, we've identified the importance of community and relationship building when working with students who don't all share the same physical classroom space. We've noticed that virtual contexts can already result in individuals feeling less connected to one another than they might feel in face-to-face settings, so we've made it a priority to be intentional about building communities with our students in order to help students feel comfortable in the learning environment. By building this sense of community, we can help our students achieve the many social and academic benefits that the research cited in this section indicates correspond with a strong learning environment. We strongly believe that constructing a cohesive community is an extremely meaningful aspect of remote and virtual learning. In the next section, we look at an example from Jennifer's work building community with students in her middle school English classes.

Instructional Snapshot: An Example From Jennifer's Work

To begin class, I use a question of the day. I try to make these questions themed, maybe related to an upcoming event, season, or news topic. I prepare the questions for the month in Google Slides. Creating them in Slides allows for easy editing if something does happen that we need to do an informal check on, such as an event in our local community or the nation. This helps our class build camaraderie as it shows this is a safe place where discussion is welcome and each student is cared for. This is important to model, and once the questions are in your class routine, they only take a few minutes. Before beginning, be sure to set ground rules for students, such as showing respect for others and use of appropriate language and word choice.

Once a majority of students have entered Zoom (typically two to three minutes after the start of class), I share the slide with the question of the day written across it. I read the question aloud and then watch as students' answers trickle in via chat. I read these aloud as well, responding to them and encouraging conversation. Because of these questions, even students that are in person prefer to be in Zoom so that they may reply to their classmates via chat. This has allowed for dynamic conversations to occur before class has even started!

Having questions that kick off class helps me learn more about my students. Often, their responses and reactions surprise me. One question that particularly led to a passionate discussion was, "Would you rather be wealthy with no friends or have friends but no money?" Students were split evenly in their views, and this sparked an insightful discussion on values and what makes people truly happy with their lives. This helped me learn about my students' outlooks on life and what values they prioritize, and it even led to them giving me suggestions for their next writing assignment.

Key Recommendations

In this section, we describe key recommendations to keep in mind when building a cohesive and supportive learning community in remote contexts. While doing this in virtual learning situations can be challenging, these suggestions can guide you as a construct an environment in which students and teachers support one another and feel comfortable:

- Conduct informal check-ins about noncurricular topics.
- Share your own excitement, vulnerability, and personality.
- Model what curiosity and learning look like for you.
- Center students' identities and experiences in the curriculum.

By incorporating these recommendations, you'll be building a supportive community that privileges students' ideas and well-being while demonstrating behaviors that contribute to a strong learning environment. Now, let's take a look at each of these suggestions in more detail.

Recommendation One: Conduct Informal Check-Ins About Noncurricular Topics

To build the relationships that are essential to strong learning communities, we recommend having informal check-ins and exchanges with students about noncurricular topics. These interactions can take a wide range of forms, address a number of topics, and be used at a variety of times. For example, you might ask your students a fun "Question of the Day" such as "What song would you listen to on repeat for an hour?" or "If you had to eat one food every day for an entire year, what would it be?" We've also seen teachers ask daily "Would You Rather" questions about a number of engaging topics; this is another enjoyable and informal way to build a classroom community. Before some of his virtual classes, Sean has asked students questions such as "What's something you're excited for this weekend?" and "What's something that has made you happy lately?"

We recommend allowing students to choose whether they respond to these questions so the interactions have a conversational feel instead of a required one. While it's possible that only some students might answer, it's also possible that more students will participate when they feel more comfortable in the learning environment and they learn about one another's interests and ideas. Jennifer has noticed that some of the questions make students nervous to share their answers with the entire class. One positive side of a virtual classroom is that students are able to message the teacher only. Jennifer still shares all replies aloud to the rest of the class and finds that this helps other students feel more comfortable. As more answers come in, students begin to feel comfortable making their messages available for the class to read. The ability to share anonymously, only to find out that your classmates relate to your reply, has been freeing for many students and allows them to feel comfortable in class.

The answers students offer to daily questions can also be used in your instruction. This further builds a classroom community as students feel that their interests are important and valued (and they are!). For example, Jennifer uses her students' favorite artists, foods, and activities when modeling writing skills or grammar practice. When learning about comparative and superlative degrees in adjectives and adverbs, it is more interesting for students to write the correct comparative degree when the example includes two rappers they know and listen to.

Although these check-ins can take place before class sessions start, such as a voluntary question that students are invited to answer before a particular class period, you can conduct them at any time at all that works for you. You might ask check-in questions with students in the middle of a lesson when you feel their energy might be lagging or you could devote some end-of-class time to community building by chatting with them about an engaging question or idea toward the end of the instructional period. Regardless of the specific topic of the check-in or the time when it takes place, we encourage you to communicate informally with students about noncurricular topics; doing so can help you construct a close and cohesive community with and among your students.

Recommendation Two: Share Your Own Excitement, Vulnerability, and Personality

Another important step toward building a strong classroom community is sharing your own personality traits and discussing things that make you feel excited and vulnerable. Doing this, we feel, can help construct a learning environment that values and embraces authentic feelings: by sharing who we are, we teachers can help create a safe space for students who may be interested in sharing their excitements, vulnerabilities, and personalities. Especially given the uncertainties and challenges in the world, we feel it can be particularly important for us as teachers to construct inclusive and safe classrooms where we model what it looks like to share authentic concerns and interests.

We can share these aspects of our identities in a variety of ways. We can discuss key topics that interest and excite us at the beginning of the school year when introducing ourselves, but this type of authentic expression shouldn't stop there. We can talk with students before and after class about family, music, movies, sports, or anything else that helps our students see us for who we are and what we value. In addition, we can talk with students about how we're feeling about things taking place in our lives that excite us, make us nervous, and convey aspects of our identities. It's also important to note that, as English teachers, our academic subject also facilitates the sharing of personal connections—we can make connections between characters and events in literature and our lives, experiences, and interests. All these conversations and connections are aligned with the structure of remote learning: we can use our virtual learning platforms and spaces to share what matters to us, express our identities, and generally model the process of being open and authentic. By displaying aspects of our identities and selves with our students, we can work toward constructing a learning environment that privileges self-expression.

Recommendation Three: Model What Curiosity and Learning Look Like for You

This recommendation follows logically from the previous one as both address the importance of teachers modeling community-building behaviors. While Recommendation Two calls for us teachers to demonstrate and share authentic aspects of our personalities, this one discusses the process of modeling what curiosity and learning look like for us in our professional and personal lives. Doing this, we feel, can help construct a community that values inquisitive thinking and is excited about learning. Modeling our own curiosities and academic interests can be especially effective in remote learning, where our role as educators can shift a bit to even more of a learning facilitator and less of a traditional instructor that dispenses information. Since students who participate in remote instruction will have some level of access to technological devices, they can find information through these electronic resources. Because of this, it's especially important that we educators create a learning community that prioritizes and values curiosity and the process of learning of one's own interests.

There are a variety of ways to provide this model for students. One tactic that can be especially effective is to routinely discuss your goals as a reader and writer and share your progress in relation to those goals. For example, during a writing workshop, you could discuss a piece of writing you're working on, noting some things you like about it and some ways you think it could be even better. Similarly, you could share reading goals you have, such as hoping to use independent reading time to explore more of the works by a certain author or to delve more deeply into a genre. By modeling these learning goals, you'll work toward building a learning community that values learning goals and will encourage your students to do similar work in their own learning.

Another impactful way to model what curiosity and learning look like for you is to talk with your students about questions you're thinking about and topics you'd like to explore further. These questions and topics can relate to something the class is studying, such as wanting to know more about something discussed in a book the class is reading (such as a time period, event, or another topic relevant to that book), but they can also take other forms. We can share with our students our curiosities about the world, such as authentic questions about human behavior, societal trends, natural phenomena, technology, or anything else that intrigues us. (We discuss the importance of curiosity and asking questions in even more detail in Chapter 6, "The Role of Inquiry in Remote Teaching and Learning.") When we talk with students about what we wonder, we can help construct a learning community that privileges curiosity and consists of members who share their ideas and wonderings through virtual communication.

Recommendation Four: Center Students' Identities and Experiences in the Curriculum

In order for us teachers to create supportive and inclusive virtual learning communities, it's essential that we use our instruction center students' identities and experiences in the curriculum. By designing learning activities that provide authentic opportunities for students to share their lived experiences and identities, we can build culturally relevant (Ladson-Billings, 1995) and culturally sustaining (Paris, 2012) learning communities that privilege students' cultures and backgrounds and use those attributes to facilitate their learning (Gay, 2002). When we position our students' identities as central to their learning, we communicate an important message to them by showing them we value their unique perspectives and see those components as central to their experiences in school.

A learning community that centers students' identities and experiences in the curriculum can take a number of forms, many of which are explored in even more depth in Chapter 5, "Culturally Relevant and Sustaining Teaching and Learning in Remote Contexts." When building a remote environment that values these components, we encourage you to actively look for opportunities for students to authentically incorporate aspects of their lives in learning activities. For example, if you're talking with students about that writing strategy of using sensory details, you can ask students to find examples of this concept in books, songs, social media posts, and other texts that they encounter in their out-of-school lives. Similarly, if your students are working on word roots, they can identify examples of words they encounter outside of school that contain these roots. In addition, it's important that we allow students to read books that represent them—and to make their own choices about which books represent them—so that they can have opportunities to see themselves in the school curriculum (Bishop, 1990). These instructional practices not only create inclusive learning environments but also can be easily implemented in remote instruction: distance learning is very conducive to student choice, relevance, and agency as students can select books and other texts that represent them and then share their selections with the class in virtual contexts.

Adapting for a Range of Modalities

We know that remote and distance learning takes a wide range of forms and is conducted using a variety of modalities. In this section, we describe key ideas to consider when implementing the chapter's insights in different forms of remote instruction, focusing specifically on entirely remote instruction (in which instruction is completely virtual), hybrid instruction (in which students are physically present in the classroom some days and engage through virtual learning other days), and hyflex instruction (in which some students are physically present in the classroom and other students join at the same time virtually). While many of the community-building recommendations described in this chapter are applicable regardless of the learning modality, we share some important points to keep in mind related to each instructional form.

Instructional Modality	Key Suggestions to Consider
Entirely remote	Use the features of remote learning to work for you as you build a community: utilize online tools such as the Zoom chat box, Google Docs, and Google Slides to communicate with your students, share information that is relevant to you, and create opportunities to do the same.
Hybrid	Remember that in hybrid instruction, you will be constructing two communities: the online community and the face-to-face version. Some of the features of the face-to-face community may not transfer to the online version and vice versa. Because of this, we recommend using both in-person and online community-building strategies. For example, you can use the features of remote learning described in the previous suggestion to construct an online learning community while using face-to-face interactions and conversations to create a cohesive face-to-face learning environment.
Hyflex	Since the hyflex format involves engaging with students through online and in-person instruction at the same time, it's important to construct a learning community that provides equal opportunities for participation and engagement with both audiences. For example, when checking in with students or modeling your ideas, be sure that you're communicating in ways to which both groups can feel connected. This can sometimes be as simple as making sure you make eye contact with the students in the class and with the camera that corresponds with what virtual students see. You can also share information through formats that all students can access whether they are in the classroom or in another setting; Google Docs and Google Slides can facilitate these interactions.

＃ 2

Class Discussion and Student Collaboration in a New Era

The ideas in this chapter extend from the insights presented in Chapter 1. While that chapter described the process of constructing a learning community in remote instruction, this chapter discusses important classroom activities that are facilitated by a strong learning community: class discussion and student collaboration. These instructional tactics, which we consider essential to effective English language arts instruction, can be challenging to implement in remote learning but are especially significant to maximizing students' learning experiences (Hurst, Wallace, & Nixon, 2013; Kyei-Blankson, Ntuli, & Donnelly, 2019). We first explore what it means to facilitate class discussion and student collaboration in the new era of remote instruction, noting specific attributes, challenges, and opportunities associated with these activities. Next, we reflect on why class discussion and student collaboration in remote learning are so important, which we follow with an instructional snapshot section that provides an example of Jennifer's work with her middle school students. Then we share key recommendations for teachers to consider when facilitating class discussions and student collaboration in remote English instruction. Finally, we discuss how the ideas described in this chapter can be utilized and adapted for a wide range of modalities.

What Does It Mean to Facilitate Class Discussion and Student Collaboration in Remote Instruction?

Remote learning has caused us English language arts teachers to rethink the concepts of discussion and collaboration. When we (Sean and Jennifer) constructed our pre-pandemic in-person learning environments, we did so with the idea that students would be able to see one other in person during discussions and that they'd be able to be positioned relatively closely (such as at the same table or desk cluster) during collaborative work. Once we moved to remote instruction, we knew we needed to make important decisions about discussion and collaboration that were informed by the features of remote learning and by our beliefs about effective teaching. Based on our beliefs that discussion and collaboration are essential aspects of English language arts instruction, we looked for methods and practices to ensure that our students could still discuss their insights and work together on relevant activities in remote contexts.

While we knew that some aspects of remote discussion and collaboration would be different, we wanted to ensure that our learning environments maintained certain key attributes of these components:

- We wanted students to be able to express their ideas with classmates in ways that foster an inclusive and open classroom environment.
- We wanted students to be able to learn from one another and to continue to develop their abilities to thoughtfully respond to others' perspectives.
- We wanted students to benefit academically, socially, and personally from collaborative work by participating in communal processes of meaning-making, communicating, and benefiting from their classmates' insights.

In order to put these principles into action in remote learning, we reflected on concepts such as our students' access to technological resources, the instructional modalities our schools were using, and the tools that we felt would best allow us to facilitate meaningful collaboration and discussion. Using collaborative tools such as Google Docs and Slides, Zoom features such as chat functions and breakout groups, and asynchronous online discussions, we created a variety of opportunities for our students to engage in inclusive, supportive, and academically meaningful collaboration.

We knew that constructing opportunities for our students to discuss course material and work collaboratively would be a challenge, but we felt it was an essential aspect of an effective English language arts learning instruction. These resources and tools provided us with a number of opportunities to create student-centered discussion opportunities for our students as they interacted with and learned from one another. In the next section, we reflect further on why class discussion and student collaboration are so important to effective remote teaching and learning of English language arts.

Why Is This Important?

Class discussion and student collaboration are important to strong remote English language arts instruction for a number of research-based reasons that are immediately applicable to teaching in today's context. First, it's important to note that discussion and collaboration have been shown to increase students' learning in English language arts in a range of ways, as these experiences promote problem-solving abilities, enhance comprehension, develop social skills, and help students develop other important abilities (Hurst et al., 2013). The effect of these activities on students' learning experiences illustrates that we educators can maximize the benefits of the work we do with our students when we create opportunities for them to work together and share ideas.

Another point of particular significance to this chapter and to today's educational context is that collaboration, interaction, and discussion are especially important to the quality of students' experiences in remote instruction (Kyei-Blankson et al., 2019). Kyei-Blankson and colleagues (2019) discuss the importance of encouraging and cultivating students' "social presence" in online learning, explaining that "social presence occurs when the learners are able to project themselves in the course as real people interacting with other members" (p. 53). By creating opportunities for students in our English language arts classes to work collaboratively, share insights, and discuss their insights, we can help maximize their social presence, which will maximize their abilities to learn and the effectiveness of their experiences.

It's also important to point out that remote collaboration and discussion has features and benefits that are not present in the traditional face-to-face version of these practices; for example, asynchronous communication and discussion (such as the kinds facilitated by online discussion boards) give students the opportunity to work through ideas at their own pace and center students, instead of the teacher, in the communication that takes place (Grisham & Wolsey, 2006). In addition, other forms of remote discussion and interaction can provide similar benefits by circumventing the typical classroom communication dynamic: when students share ideas remotely through Zoom features such as chat boxes and breakout rooms and Google programs such as Google Docs and Slides, they do not need to have the same level of comfort with in-person communication. Students may or may not be comfortable with sharing ideas verbally in the traditional classrooms setting for a variety of reasons, such as the size of the class, their confidence in the material, the amount of time available, and their previous experiences in school, and variety of personal attributes; the technology-based interaction and collaboration made necessary by remote instruction can provide all students with varied, decentralized, democratic, and differentiated opportunities to discuss ideas and collaborate with their peers (Rhine & Bailey, 2011).

To maximize our students' learning experiences (in English language arts, in general, and in remote instruction, in particular), it's essential that we create opportunities for our students to collaborate with one another and discuss their insights. In the next section, we look at an example of Jennifer's work facilitating interaction and collaboration in her middle school English classes.

Instructional Snapshot: An Example From Jennifer's Work

Student collaboration and productivity intimidated me the most when remote learning began. English is a difficult content to grasp for most of us, and to ensure students' understanding in a remote setting seemed a daunting challenge. Although it is a challenge, I would remove the adjective *daunting* and replace it with *innovative*. Students' participation in their learning and collaboration has been transformed to become more inclusive and less intimidating. As said previously, the traditional classroom setting has its own set of barriers that remote learning has knocked down.

First, it is important to highlight the mighty Zoom chat. Zoom places the user in control and allows them to send chats privately to the host (the teacher/co-teachers) or publicly to all in the session. With remote learning, all our verbal discussions are happening via video calls or video chat boxes and the private chat feature allows students to participate without the pressure of being wrong in front of peers. This allows me to read all answers, public and private, and verbally confirm or redirect the answers provided. This creates a foundation for conversation and collaboration to continue.

Creating a collaborative conversation can be as simple as students replying with their opinion or answer to a small, short question. For example, while reading Edgar Allen Poe's "Tell-Tale Heart," I asked students to send a "Y" in the chat if they believed the main character could truly hear the old man's heart and an "N" if he could not. By starting with a simple question, students were more inclined to participate and, in turn, continued participating as they had a stake in the conversation at hand. Collaboration then ensued as students saw their classmates' responses and, without facilitation, began pulling details from the text that proved they were right or sent their inferences of what the character is hearing (if he is indeed not hearing the old man's heart). I will note that it is important to provide prompting questions as the students engage in discussion in order to guide them, especially if the goal is to use a collaborative discussion to demonstrate the students' understanding of the daily learning objective.

The crowned collaboration innovator, Google, is not new to remote engagement or learning. Google products, such as Docs and Slides, are key players in the success of a remote classroom. Docs and Slides, when students are not signed into their Google accounts, allow students to type anonymously. For discussions where the goal is to collaborate and foster creativity, the ability for students to participate anonymously is conducive for both teacher and student. Collaborative activities that can be done via Google Slides and Docs could be a plot diagram, a brainstorm for a writing prompt, or a class diagram to practice parts of speech. When it is necessary to track participation, the teacher can ask students to sign into their Google accounts.

Using the same formats each day can be a bit repetitive and eventually become tedious. As teachers, we are always searching for ways to present content in a new, fresh way to keep learning fun and engaging. Padlet has helped me create new ways to reinvent discussion boards and avoid individual assignments. Imagine a virtual bulletin board, and that is what I find their "wall" template to be similar to. Due to its colorful background and sleek presentation, Padlet is much less intimidating than a public discussion board. Most often, I use it for students to practice writing thesis statements. I place a writing prompt as the question header and students respond to the prompt with their theses, which appear in a fashion that looks like sticky notes. Padlet is synched with Google, so if a student is logged into their student account, then their name appears when they reply to the prompt. Otherwise, students can post anonymously. I use Padlet as a way to practice lessons and discuss the responses via Zoom, offering edits or suggestions. After a few practice responses, students are instructed that their response will be graded and to write their names in their responses in order to receive credit.

Just as with an in-person classroom, the key goal when creating a remote learning and classroom plan is for students to become comfortable enough to participate without fear of rejection. This is done through the building of confidence as students learn and master the subject as well as receiving respect throughout their learning process. It is natural to be intimidated or fearful of being wrong and our goal as educators is to ensure students feel safe, welcomed, and appreciated as members of our community. As I navigate the curriculum, I find myself using these tools again and again as we begin new units or to provide students with the support they need to be successful.

Key Recommendations

In this section, we share and discuss key recommendations to consider when facilitating class discussions and student collaboration in your own remote

English language arts instruction. These suggestions are designed to help you as you put the ideas and insights described in this chapter into practice:

- Strategically utilize a wide range of collaboration and discussion methods.
- Explain both the how and the why of discussion and collaboration tools.
- Emphasize respect during student discussions and collaborations.
- Provide students with choice and ownership regarding their collaborations and discussions.

Incorporating these recommendations will help you construct interactive, thoughtful, and student-centered discussions and collaborations that will help students achieve the maximum benefit of these important activities. In addition, they will guide you as you consider how to convey your ideas and beliefs about effective English language arts discussions and collaborations to the remote context. Now, let's look at each of these suggestions in more detail.

Recommendation One: Strategically Utilize a Wide Range of Collaboration and Discussion Methods

There are two important components of this recommendation: the first is to incorporate a variety of methods when creating opportunities for students to have discussions and work collaboratively, and the second is to select those collaboration and discussion methods strategically based on how well they align with the purpose of that task. By putting these ideas into action, we ensure that we are providing our students with a wide range of ways to engage with each other and that those interaction forms are aligned with the kinds of collaboration and discussion in which they're engaging. When we're planning ways for our students to interact, we want to keep them active and engaged with a variety of methods and activities: depending, in part, on the modalities we're using, we might ask students to share responses verbally through Zoom, write a comment in a chat box, or work collaboratively on Google Docs and/or Google Slides.

However, this variety is associated with more than just keeping students interested: we also want to consider a range of collaboration and discussion options so that we can select the method that best aligns with our instructional goal. For example, we might ask students in a Zoom meeting to share a short response through the chat box, while a longer response or collaborative activity would be better suited for a Google Doc. In addition, if we want students to be able to think about classmates' responses outside of the scheduled class meeting, we can create asynchronous discussion boards that align with this purpose. By closely aligning our instructional goals with the discussion and collaboration methods we ask our students to use, we can ensure that the connection between the form and function of the tools we're using.

Recommendation Two: Explain Both the How and the Why of Discussion and Collaboration Tools

Since the collaboration and discussion tools used in remote English instruction can be unfamiliar to some students and different from what they may have previously used for these purposes, we recommend talking early in the school year with students about how to implement the discussion and collaboration tools you're utilizing. This can be done during the same time you go over other procedures and guidelines essential for student success; for example, you might introduce some of the resources and programs you'll use to facilitate collaboration and discussion, model their use for students, and provide them with some especially important tips to keep in mind when using it on their own. By doing this, we can help students feel comfortable using the resources—which can, in turn, help students feel more likely to engage during discussions and collaborations.

In addition to showing students how to implement tools and resources used for discussion and collaboration, we recommend talking with students about *why* they'll be using those tools. By sharing (in age and developmentally aligned ways) with students the reasons they'll be certain resources for particular types of discussion and collaboration, we can create an atmosphere of transparency and clear communication in our instruction. For example, before we ask students to use online discussion boards, we can share with them the benefits of using these boards and the types of discussions for which they'll use them. We can then compare that resource with another type, such as Google Slides, highlighting the kinds of collaboration for which that tool will be used. These kinds of discussions provide students with the clarity that comes from purposeful technology use (Young & Bush, 2004) and can help them feel comfortable engaging with these tools and resources during remote learning.

Recommendation Three: Emphasize Respect During Student Discussions and Collaborations

To maximize the effectiveness of students' experiences collaborating and discussing information in the remote English language arts setting, we strongly recommend emphasizing respectful and supportive communication during these collaborative activities. There are certainly legitimate concerns about young people communicating in harmful ways online, which has led to an increased focus on teaching youth about digital citizenship, which includes respectful and supportive online communication (Jones & Mitchell, 2016). Since much of remote learning, discussion, and collaboration involves the use of digital communication tools, we believe it is important for teachers to talk with students about key attributes of effective digital citizenship.

Teachers can model effective digital communication for students by showing them what respectful collaboration can look like. For instance, a teacher might respond to a student's discussion board post with an example of what a supportive and respectful reply looks like. The teacher could then think aloud for students about the comment's specific supportive and respectful aspects and then use that information to launch a conversation with students about what they can do to ensure they can respond to others in positive ways. Teachers and students could work together to create a set of expectations for respectful collaboration that can be posted on the class's learning management system (such as Blackboard, Canvas, or Google Classroom). The teacher can then periodically remind students of these expectations to help ensure respectful collaboration and discussion.

Recommendation Four: Provide Students With Choice and Ownership Regarding Their Collaborations and Discussions

In order to maximize the quality of and engagement associated with students' collaborative work and discussions, we recommend providing opportunities for choice and ownership. The choice and ownership you provide will vary based on the specific work students are doing at a particular time and can take a variety of forms, such as opportunities to choose the format through which they collaborate, the content they discuss, or a combination of the two. When providing students with choice, we believe it's important to provide a combination of teacher guidance and student freedom. In other words, we want to provide students with clear expectations for an assignment while still giving them as much opportunity as possible to individualize their work.

For example, if students are working collaboratively in a jigsaw activity in which each group shares what they noticed about a key section or story element, groups could have the opportunity to select how they collaborate and share the results of their works: they could work together and display their ideas through Google Docs, Google Slides, or another collaborative tool. They could also make choices related to the content they discuss, such as which aspects of a particular section most stood out to them and why. Similarly, we can provide students with choice and ownership in the ideas they share in whole-class discussions about texts they've read by asking them to make personal connections between their own lives, issues that matter to them, and other works they've read and the content in the pieces. In addition, since students may be more comfortable sharing these ideas through different tools and mediums, we can take this form of individualization into account by allowing students to share their ideas verbally, through a Zoom chat function, or through another tool. These opportunities for individualization can help students feel a sense of ownership over their collaboration and discussion experiences.

Adapting for a Range of Modalities

When reflecting on class discussions and opportunities for student collaboration in remote learning, it's important to consider the range of modalities through which remote English language arts instruction is conducted. In this section, we share ideas to consider when implementing the chapter's insights in different forms of remote instruction, focusing specifically on entirely remote instruction (in which instruction is completely virtual), hybrid instruction (in which students are physically present in the classroom some days and engage through virtual learning other days), and hyflex instruction (in which some students are physically present in the classroom and other students join at the same time virtually). It's important to note that the core attributes of collaboration and discussion and the key associated recommendations described in this chapter can be applied no matter the modality. The modality adaptations discussed in this section are designed to help you think through the features of the instructional format you use and how it aligns with the principles of effective collaboration and discussion.

Instructional Modality	Key Suggestions to Consider
Entirely remote	If you are teaching entirely remotely, we encourage you to reflect on all the collaboration and discussion tools available to you and your students. You might even make a list of the online tools you can have access to and are comfortable with, noting the features of those tools and the kinds of collaboration and discussion they can facilitate. In addition, since your students will be engaging with each other entirely online, we recommend spending time discussing the features of digital citizenship to ensure that students will communicate respectfully.

Instructional Modality	Key Suggestions to Consider
Hybrid	Since students in hybrid instruction will take part in virtual learning some days and in-person interaction on other days, it's important to keep both of these types of interaction in mind while planning collaboration and discussion since some discussion and collaboration methods will be more aligned with in-person discussions and others with remote idea exchanges. Because of this, we recommend being particularly strategic and mindful of the way the class is meeting when making decisions about discussion and collaboration.
Hyflex	Because hyflex instruction calls for some students to join the class online at the same time others are present in person, it's important to keep both groups of students in mind when constructing opportunities for collaboration and discussion. There are multiple ways that we educators can do this; one tactic is to create opportunities for all students in the course (whether they join a particular meeting through an online platform like Zoom or if they're present in person) to use technological collaboration tools like Google Docs and Google Slides to interact. This can allow all students in the class to work collaboratively and maximize the opportunities for discussion among the students.

II

The Potential of Remote ELA Instruction

3

A New Format of Writing and Grammar Instruction

In this chapter, we look closely at the best ways to teach writing and grammar in the context of remote English language arts instruction. While teaching writing and grammar remotely can certainly be challenging, we also feel that the remote environment provides a number of opportunities for innovative and engaging instruction in this aspect of English language arts. Through the information in this chapter, we convey essential aspects of effective writing and grammar instruction and provide suggestions to consider when working with your students remotely on these instructional components. We begin this chapter by first exploring key components of remote writing and grammar instruction, identifying its major attributes and the challenges and opportunities associated with it. Next, we reflect on why it's so important to effectively teach grammar and writing in remote contexts, which we follow with an instructional snapshot section that provides an example of Jennifer's work with her middle school students. Then we share key recommendations for teachers to consider when teaching writing and grammar remotely. Finally, we discuss how the ideas in this chapter can be implemented in a range of modalities.

What Are the Key Aspects of Remote Writing and Grammar Instruction?

When we reflect on effective writing and grammar instruction, we think of an active process for students and teachers. We picture strategy-focused mini-lessons, discussions of mentor texts, engaged students working on drafts, conferences between students and teachers, and other demonstrations of active learning. While the specific methods of delivery and collaboration will certainly differ, we feel that all these components of effective writing instruction can be achieved in remote learning. Through the purposeful and strategic use of technological resources, we educators can provide students with writing instruction that represents its research-based best practices. We believe remote teaching and learning can align with key components of student-centered writing instruction: remote instruction that utilizes short, focused periods of direct instruction on a platform such as Google Meet or Zoom, followed by opportunities for students to work on their own pieces of writing allows students to engage in writing instruction in active ways.

For example, in their book *Writing Workshop: The Essential Guide*, Fletcher and Portalupi (2001) compare strong writing instruction to an industrial arts class or to ski lessons in which the instructor models and explains a concept or strategy and then creates opportunities for the students to try it out on their own, checking in with them individually while doing so. Remote writing and grammar instruction, we believe, can provide this same student-focused context in which our students work on their writing and teachers check in with and support them as they do so. The modalities might be different than what many of us are used to, but we can still apply the principles of strong writing instruction to remote learning. When teaching grammatical concepts in the context of writing instruction, for instance, we educators can apply the same best practices of focused mini-lessons and mentor text use that we would apply in the face-to-face classroom. In this chapter, we further explore the significance of these instructional practices and ways to put them into action in the English classroom.

Why Is It Important?

While there are certainly challenges associated with it, we strongly believe in the importance of remote instruction that aligns with the best practices of teaching writing and grammar. By creating opportunities for our students to examine mentor texts, apply writing strategies in authentic ways, receive individualized instruction from us, and share work with real-world audiences, we can provide students with outstanding writing instruction, which is essential to students' success in many aspects of their lives (National Writing Project & Nagin, 2006). In the book *Because Writing Matters*, the National Writing Project and Carl Nagin (2006) assert that effective writing instruction is so important to our students for a range of reasons: "in today's increasingly diverse society, writing is a gateway for success in academia, the new workplace, and the global economy, as well as for our collective success as a participatory democracy" (p. 2).

Additional resources published since *Because Writing Matters* continue to comment and elaborate on the importance of effective writing skills in today's society; for example, the 2016 National Council of Teachers of English (NCTE) document *Professional Knowledge for the Teaching of Writing* explains that our students' writing skills are essential to their successes in a number of important contexts. Among the ideas in this NCTE piece that highlight the significance of writing to our students' lives are assertions that writing in today's society takes a number of forms, writing is done for audiences and purposes beyond school, students' abilities to write are important to their abilities to participate in society, writing can be used to enhance students' personal growth, and digital environments have created new audiences and opportunities for writing. Now, in today's world, we can put the research-based insights in *Because Writing Matters* and NCTE's *Professional Knowledge for the Teaching of Writing* into action by connecting them with the features and attributes of remote learning. By providing our students with strong remote writing instruction that applies the best practices of teaching writing to distance learning, we can help them develop essential skills for their personal, academic, and career success.

Now, let's take a look at an example of Jennifer's work with the students in her middle school English class as she engages them in remote writing instruction.

Instructional Snapshot: An Example From Jennifer's Work

In Virginia, eighth-grade students take a state writing test. Much of our year is spent exploring the types of writing tested: expository, argumentative, and persuasive. The mentor texts most often used are essays from authors or peers.

As the state test drew near, our class spent time reviewing templar essays. Before beginning, the lesson's focus was defined. On this specific day, hooks and bridges were reviewed. The lesson opened with students defining what hooks and bridges are, their purpose, and where they belong in an essay. After that, students joined my session on Pear Deck.

I had created a Google Slides presentation that contained templar essays for us to review and identify parts as a class. Because we had defined what a hook and a bridge were, we began reading the essays one at a time. Students were prompted to answer questions as we read. The two questions that are asked first during our writing lessons are, "What question is the author answering?" and "What is the author's thesis?" The questions that followed asked students to identify what sentences made up the hook and which were to be identified as the essay's bridge. These questions would be answered for each of the three templar essays to ensure the students achieved mastery.

After the Google Slides were presented, students were assigned an independent practice. Students were required to write an introductory paragraph using completed brainstorms, written prior to the lesson by me. Depending on the student's tier level, they had an option of which brainstorm to use; tier one students had an option of three brainstorms to choose from while tier three students were assigned one brainstorm. Allowing students to choose what brainstorm to use gave them control over the prompt they wrote about, thereby increasing student engagement and productivity. This independent practice was done using Google Docs, making it easy for me to monitor progress.

While the students worked independently on Zoom, I was able to visit their documents and see their work. I left comments of encouragement and notes on what to improve and how to. I spoke out on Zoom, asking students to message me if they needed me to review their writing with them, and monitored the classroom to check on in-person students' work. Students reached out using the private chat tool on Zoom, allowing me to immediately visit their Doc and provide guidance.

The lesson ended with me instructing students to submit their work. I reviewed their hook and bridges to assess for mastery. Although this lesson was not a mini-lesson, the topic was reviewed the following week as a mini-lesson. The same format could be followed for a mini-lesson, with the Slides being shortened or the independent practice being done on the Slides versus externally.

Key Recommendations

In this section, we provide and describe key recommendations to keep in mind regarding remote writing and grammar instruction. Following these suggestions will help you put the best practices of teaching writing and grammar into action in remote contexts, providing your students with the instruction, insights, and support that will help them write effectively:

- ◆ Conduct short, focused mini-lessons on the features of specific writing strategies and grammatical concepts.

- Use mentor texts to illustrate how published authors use these strategies and concepts authentically.
- Help students analyze the importance of writing strategies and grammatical concepts to effective writing.
- Use technological collaboration tools to confer with students as they apply writing strategies and grammatical concepts to their own works.
- Ask students to reflect on how specific strategies and concepts enhance the effectiveness of their writings.

By utilizing these ideas, you'll provide your students with strategic writing instruction that presents key strategies and concepts as tools for effective writing, purposefully utilizes mentor texts, creates opportunities for students to apply writing strategies and concepts to their own works, and helps students reflect on the impact these writing tools have on their own works. Now, we describe these recommendations in more detail, discussing their applications to remote teaching and learning.

Recommendation One: Conduct Short, Focused Mini-Lessons on the Features of Specific Writing Strategies and Grammatical Concepts

We recommend beginning the process of effective remote grammar and writing instruction with short, focused mini-lessons on specific strategies and concepts. Whether we deliver these mini-lessons synchronously through live instruction on a platform like Google Meet or Zoom or asynchronously through a recorded video that we create and make available for our students (or a combination of both, such as a live lesson on Zoom that we record for students to have access to later), we can use these brief and informative explanations to introduce students to important components of effective writing and describe for them the key features of those strategies. Regardless of the specific modality used to remotely present these mini-lessons, we suggest using the mini-lessons to describe to students what a particular writing strategy or grammatical concept is and why it is important to effective writing. This instructional approach will help students see these strategies and concepts as tools of strong writing, thereby preparing them for the subsequent steps of the instructional process in which students ultimately apply the strategies they learn to their own works and reflect on those strategies' impacts.

As you prepare the mini-lessons, you'll present to your students, we recommend structuring the content of each lesson in three sections: (1) What is the writing strategy or grammatical concept being discussed? (2) What are its key features? and (3) Why is it important to effective writing? The first question is not only the most fundamental, as it focuses on what the mini-lesson is describing, but also very important, because by clearly identifying the topic of a mini-lesson while planning it, we can ensure that we're giving students clear and focused instruction that addresses a specific aspect of writing. For example, a strong mini-lesson on sensory detail would clearly identify its focal topic and convey that topic to students early in the lesson. The second question calls for us as teachers to explain to students the essential aspects of the lesson's topic to students. Continuing with the example of sensory detail, a lesson on this topic would describe for students in clear and concise ways what sensory detail is, providing information on the ways authors use language to appeal to readers' senses. Finally, the third question helps build students' understandings of the significance of the focal concept by sharing reasons authors might use the topic to maximize the effectiveness of their works. When describing sensory language, for example, we can share with students some reasons why authors choose to use that concept, focusing on ideas such as the ways it allows readers to deeply understand a particular scene or event in ways that stand out to them.

Recommendation Two: Use Mentor Texts to Illustrate How Published Authors Use These Strategies and Concepts Authentically

Once you've shared with students a brief mini-lesson that focuses on the key aspects of a particular writing strategy or grammatical concept, we recommend building on that information by sharing with students one or more published mentor texts in which the focal strategy is effectively used. Sharing published examples of key writing strategies and grammatical concepts provides students with a number of important benefits: (1) It provides them with concrete examples of what specific writing strategies and grammatical concepts look like in authentic situations. (2) It can increase students' "buy-in" to the concept or strategy by showing them that it is used in real-world contexts, not just in classroom activities or on worksheets. (3) It can further engage students in the material, especially when they examine examples from texts that are of high interest to them.

When selecting examples to share with your students, we encourage you to ask yourself three questions: (1) Is it a clear example of the focal writing strategy or grammatical concept? (2) Is the example from a text aligned with the students' general reading level? and (3) Is the example from a text that students in the class may find interesting, relevant, or engaging? If you can answer yes to these three questions, then that text would be a great mentor text to use with your students! For example, you might select the following example from Pablo Cartaya's (2017) novel *The Epic Fail of Arturo Zamora*—in which the book's protagonist Arturo describes his family's restaurant—as an example of sensory detail if you feel the text is aligned with your students' general reading level and potentially engaging to them:

> And there it was: our colorful sign. The *o* in *Cocina* was bright orange while the rest of the letters were outlined in green and black, and behind the letters was the faint shape of an island. Two multicolored giraffes greeted customers at the entrance of the restaurant, making an arch as you walked through the French double doors.
>
> (p. 18)

The sensory details in this passage provide a clear model of what this writing strategy looks like in the context of a published text, which can help convey to students the role the strategy plays in authentic writing done by published authors.

There are a variety of ways to use the features of remote learning to share mentor texts with students. As with the mini-lessons described in the previous recommendation, we teachers can share these texts synchronously through a format such as Zoom or Google Meet, asynchronously through a recorded video, or through a combination (such as a live lesson that is recorded and made available for reference later on). When sharing mentor texts remotely, we recommend placing the text of the selected passage on your screen by either transcribing it or sharing an image of the text and sharing the screen with your students. As you share these examples, we advise reading the passage aloud as your students follow along. While doing so, we suggest thinking aloud for your students about how the author uses the focal concept or strategy, modeling your thought process about what you notice regarding the author's use of the strategy, the impact it has on the effectiveness of the piece, and why you think the author chose to use that concept. Doing this will give students an example of how to look at and reflect on a mentor text that effectively uses a specific writing strategy. This knowledge will prepare students for the third component of this instructional process, described in the next recommendation.

Recommendation Three: Help Students Analyze the Importance of Writing Strategies and Grammatical Concepts to Effective Writing

At this stage of the instructional process, students work to analyze the importance of the focal strategy to effective writing. While you'll still provide students with support and guidance, this step gives increased ownership and responsibility to students: it represents a shift from the teacher discussing the features and impact of a particular writing strategy or grammatical concept to the students analyzing its significance. While there are a variety of ways to organize the specifics of this activity based on particular instructional modalities and other aspects, the core components are that students look at a published text, analyze the author's use of the focal strategy, and reflect on how and why the author chose to use that strategy.

Because of the many ways students can engage in this activity, it aligns well with remote learning. For example, you might share with your students an electronic file of a short story and ask each student to select an example of the strategy or concept on which you're focusing that day. This activity can also be easily done in groups: students could use Zoom breakout rooms or a similar resource to work together to find examples and analyze the importance of the focal strategy. When facilitating group work on this activity, you could provide each group with a separate text or have all the groups use the same text for the activity.

We recommend implementing this activity in a variety of ways to keep students engaged and to demonstrate all the different ways that this type of analysis can take place. In addition, creating a range of opportunities for students to analyze writing strategies and grammatical concepts will allow them to purposefully use the tools of remote learning in a number of context-specific ways, giving them a range of opportunities to engage with content and with varying technological resources. Whether students work independently or in groups, we suggest asking them to share their findings at the conclusion of the activity. This celebrates students' work, allows students to learn from each other, and creates opportunities for you as the teacher to address any misunderstandings or confusion.

The graphic organizer depicted in Figure 3.1 (also available in Appendix A) provides a useful resource for students as they analyze the importance of a writing strategy or grammatical concept to the effectiveness of a published text. We recommend making electronic copies of the resource available for students so they can use it to record their identifications and insights while working on this activity.

Text You Used	Example of the Focal Strategy or Concept in the Text	Why You Feel the Strategy or Concept Is Important to the Effectiveness of the Text

Figure 3.1 Graphic Organizer for Published Text Analysis

Recommendation Four: Use Technological Collaboration Tools to Confer With Students as They Apply Writing Strategies and Grammatical Concepts to Their Own Works

Now that students have learned about the features of key writing strategies and grammatical concepts, examined mentor texts, and analyzed the importance of focal strategies and concepts to published examples, it's time to provide them with an opportunity to put the ideas they've learned into practice in their own writing! To do this, we recommend creating instructional time dedicated to students working on their own writing projects. Building this independent writing time into your instruction gives them time to use the writing strategies and grammatical concepts they've been learning about it in class. In addition, it varies the instructional modality moving away from a typical Zoom- or Google Meet–style lesson and to a writing workshop structure that focuses on students' individual works as writers. Depending on your curriculum, the projects students create during this time can be works of students' choice, assigned topics, or a combination of the two.

Regardless of the specific pieces they are writing, we suggest holding individual conferences with students to monitor their progress and provide individualized instruction (Myroup, 2020). In these conferences, we recommend talking with each student about the piece they're writing, asking them questions about their goals for the work, noting its specific strengths, and identifying a specific way for the writer to continue to develop it. We suggest incorporating the focal strategy or concept that the class has been discussing into the conference conversation but not limiting the discussion to that topic. Instead, we encourage you to look at all aspects of each student's work so that you can provide each of them with specific and individualized insights about their writing.

One-on-one writing conferences can still be effectively utilized in remote learning, although they will take somewhat different forms than they would in an in-person, non–socially distanced classroom. Instead of sitting down at a table with a student to hold a conference, we can use technological collaboration tools to adapt our conferences for remote learning. One effective tactic for holding remote writing conferences with students is to place each student in their own Zoom breakout room during their independent writing time. Then, to confer with a student, you'll join their individual breakout room and hold a one-on-one conference with them about the piece they're writing. We like this method of conferring because of the opportunities it provides for conversation and clarification. If you're unable to communicate with students through a platform like Zoom because of technological issues, another way to hold a remote conference is by using Google Docs to have a text-based conversation in which you ask them questions about their work, identify specific strengths, and note particular suggestions for improvement. If you use this text-based model, we encourage you to be sure to communicate with students about their work by asking them questions and waiting for responses before giving them suggestions for improvement; this exchange of ideas can help you understand students' goals and interests, which can allow you to individualize your feedback to that individual student.

Regardless of the specific technological tools used in a one-on-one writing conference, we recommend using a graphic organizer to record the information discussed in the conference and keep track of student progress. You can keep an electronic file for each student containing the graphic organizer from each conference you had with them, which will provide a great deal of formative assessment data and documentation of their writing development. One example of a graphic organizer you could use for this purpose is depicted in Figure 3.2; this organizer asks for the student's name, the date, day's focal strategy, the title and a brief description of the piece the student is writing, a strength of the piece you identified, and a concrete suggestion for improvement you shared with the student.

Student's name:

Date:

The day's focal strategy:

Title and Brief Description of the Student's Piece	A Specific Strength of the Piece You Identified	A Concrete Suggestion for Improvement You Shared With the Student

Figure 3.2 Writing Conference Graphic Organizer

Recommendation Five: Ask Students to Reflect on How Specific Strategies and Concepts Enhance the Effectiveness of Their Writings

We recommend concluding these steps by asking students to reflect on the focal strategy on which you and the students have been focusing throughout the instructional process. To facilitate students' reflections, we suggest asking them two related questions, each one designed to promote thoughtful analysis of the importance of specific grammatical concepts and writing strategies to effective writing. First, we recommend asking students how the focal strategy enhanced the writing they did that day. For example, if the class was focused on the use of sensory detail, you could ask the students, "How did the sensory details you used in your piece enhance the effectiveness of your work?" In addition, we suggest asking students to reflect on how they think their work would be different if they didn't use the focal strategy. When studying sensory detail, you might ask, "How do you think your piece would be different if you didn't use sensory detail in it?" By responding to these questions, students will think carefully and analytically about the impact of the focal writing strategy or grammatical concept, which can help them further understand how that strategy or concept can function as a tool that writers use to enhance the quality of their works.

There are a variety of ways students can share these reflections while utilizing the features of remote learning. One especially effective practice is to ask students to use a shared Google Doc to share their responses. After students reflect individually on the questions, they can look at their peers' answers and note similarities and differences between their insights on the importance of the focal strategy and their classmates' ideas. Once they've done that, students can interact further with their peers by writing positive comments under their classmates' responses, such as similarities in the responses or new ideas they gained from someone else's insights. If you would prefer students respond to you individually, you can ask them to submit these ideas directly to you through an assignment in your learning management system, such as Canvas, Blackboard, Google Classroom, or another similar system. No matter how you organize students' submissions, these reflection questions will help students reflect on the importance of key writing strategies and grammatical concepts while also providing a meaningful sense of closure to this instructional process.

Adapting for a Range of Modalities

Since remote English language arts instruction is conducted by different individuals using a range of modalities, this section shares ideas to consider when implementing this chapter's insights on effective writing and grammar instruction in varying forms of remote instruction. In it, we describe insights to consider when implementing the chapter's points about effective writing and grammar instruction in a range of modes: entirely remote instruction (in which instruction is completely virtual), hybrid instruction (in which students are physically present in the classroom some days and engage through virtual learning other days), and hyflex instruction (in which some students are physically present in the classroom and other students join at the same time virtually). The modality adaptations discussed here are designed to provide you with additional support and recommendations as you help your students understand that writing strategies and grammar concepts are tools that authors use purposefully to maximize the impacts of their works.

Instructional Modality	Key Suggestions to Consider
Entirely remote	Entirely remote writing instruction aligns with a variety of ways for students to use technological tools and resources to learn, collaborate, and share. We encourage you to think about the online tools to which you have access, with which you are comfortable, and that will facilitate the instructional components of this process. For instance, we suggest identifying the best ways for you to deliver remote mini-lessons and mentor text explanations, the collaboration tools that you think will most effectively allow your students to work together on text analyses, and the technological resources that will best facilitate individual writing conferences. As you select these technological tools, we encourage you to keep in mind that some students may have varying levels of internet access, so there may be situations in which you might need to choose alternative options that do not require high-speed internet.
Hybrid	Because students engaging in hybrid instruction participate in virtual learning on some days and in-person classes on others, the most important aspect of planning for this modality is to reflect on which strategies and tools align best with in-person instruction and which ones work best for online learning. For example, if you are conducting an in-person mini-lesson on the key features of a grammatical concept or writing strategy, you'll want to select resources and tactics aligned with that implementation strategy. If students are participating in remote learning when discussing the importance of a focal strategy to a published text, you'll want to organize that activity in ways that correspond with the characteristics of remote learning.

Instructional Modality	Key Suggestions to Consider
Hyflex	We believe that strong hyflex writing instruction keeps in mind the components of this unique instructional modality. Since hyflex instruction calls for some students to join the class online at the same time others are present in person, we encourage you to incorporate both groups into your writing instruction. When you're conducting direct instruction through the form of a mini-lesson or mentor text explanation, we suggest doing so in a way that is accessible to students in the classroom and those joining via Zoom or a similar platform by live broadcasting the lesson and recording it for students joining online. During activities in which students share their insights with each other, we recommend using technological resources such as Google Docs that will allow all students to collaborate and share their ideas in common ways. Similarly, during writing conferences, you can use the same format whether students are present in person or online so that all students will have the same opportunities for interaction with the teacher.

4

Literature Instruction in the Remote Environment

In this chapter, we explore the most effective ways to engage students in literature instruction in remote contexts, identifying important and essential aspects of teaching literature and reflecting on engaging and meaningful ways to apply those instructional principles to remote English language arts instruction. As with the ideas we explored in the previous chapter on effective writing instruction, we believe that there are a variety of ways to use the tools of remote learning to implement the practices of effective literature instruction. We examine in this chapter key aspects of strong literature instruction, and then we share insights to consider when remotely engaging your students in these practices. First, we describe key components of strong remote literature instruction, noting major features and challenges associated with it. Then, we discuss why it's so important to effectively teach literature in remote contexts, which we follow with an instructional snapshot section that provides an example of Jennifer's work with her middle school students. Afterward, we share recommendations for teachers to consider when teaching literature remotely. Finally, we discuss how the ideas in this chapter can be implemented in a range of modalities.

What Are the Key Aspects of Remote Literature Instruction?

In their book *Bridging English*, Milner, Milner, and Mitchell (2012) identify three phrases of teaching literature: enter, explore, and extend. These three components of literature instruction work together to provide students with engaging, thought-provoking, relevant, and meaningful experiences with works of literature they read. We believe that these instructional strategies can be effectively implemented in remote learning. In this section, we discuss key aspects of Milner, Milner, and Mitchell's three stages of teaching literature and offer our insights into the ways each of these instructional stages can be connected to remote learning.

The Enter Stage

In the "enter" stage, students engage in activities designed to activate their prior knowledge about key issues in the text and provide student-centered entry points to their works. According to Milner et al. (2012), "[t]hese activities can take many forms; but all are designed to activate students' thoughts, experiences, and feelings about something essential in the text that follows or to build background knowledge necessary for reading it" (p. 121). By using instructional practices that connect to our students' insights and establish understandings of relevant contextual information, we can help our students begin their reading experiences in engaging and meaningful ways.

Connecting the Enter Stage to Remote Instruction

The features and tools of remote instruction provide a number of engaging and meaningful opportunities for students to "enter" a piece of literature. For example, we English teachers can ask students to use Google Docs to write reflections on key issues that they'll encounter in a text: if a book relates to the importance of challenging societal assumptions, we can ask students to reflect on societal assumptions they have challenged or would like to challenge. This experience can activate students' prior knowledge of the topic and provide them with an accessible point of entry into the text. Students can then use the Google Doc responses to read one another's ideas and note connections between their peers' ideas and their own. There are a number of other ways to use collaboration and instruction tools featured in remote instruction to help students initially engage with and reflect on key ideas in a work of literature, such as student groups creating Google Slides about contextual information that will help the class access the piece. While specific practices and tools will vary, we educators can use features of remote learning to provide our students with useful points of entry into a literary work.

The Explore Stage

The "explore" stage of literature instruction focuses on student "response, interpretation, formal analysis, and critical synthesis" (Milner et al., 2012, p. 122). There are a variety of ways we English language arts teachers can facilitate students' interpretations and analysis; Milner, Milner, and Mitchell advise us to focus on students' unique responses and reactions to literature by prioritizing activities and instructional practices that center students in the curriculum. These practices can help students connect to and analyze literature on their own instead of viewing literary analysis as a teacher-directed activity in which students' individual insights are not relevant. By emphasizing our students' unique responses, these authors explain, we can help facilitate explorations of literature that are meaningful to them.

Connecting the Explore Stage to Remote Instruction
Remote instruction provides a range of ways for students to explore literary texts in the student-centered ways that Milner et al. (2012) describe. Students can use remote learning tools to respond to a text individually, analyze them collaboratively, and develop their own conclusions. The specific instructional tools you use will certainly vary based on the nature of the activities and the resources that you feel are best aligned with what you want your students to do. For example, when students make personal connections to a text, they can respond using tools that facilitate the types of connections they're being asked to make: shorter, more immediate responses could be shared through quick-access features like the Zoom chat box, while longer responses can be better fits for online discussion boards. Similarly, students can use a variety of collaboration methods that fit particular group activities, such as discussing ideas in Zoom breakout rooms or creating more developed collaborative responses through tools such as Google Docs or Google Slides. Finally, in situations in which students conduct their own independent analyses of literary works, we recommend providing brief mini-lessons that explain key features of those analyses and discuss important strategies to use while creating them. Then you can hold one-on-one virtual conferences with students as they work on these pieces.

The Extend Stage
In the "extend" stage of literature instruction, students take the responses, ideas, and analyses they've developed in the first two stages and use those insights to connect the text to the world around them. Milner et al. (2012) explain "the extension phrase should lift students beyond an egocentric focus and into an awareness of themselves within larger social, cultural, political, and moral worlds" (p. 122). When engaging in extension activities, students can use the text as a point of entry that facilitates their reflections of the types of "worlds" and issues that Milner, Milner, and Mitchell describe. These activities highlight the essentialness of literature because of the way it can help us reflect on not only the text itself but the world around us as well. In addition,

extension activities that facilitate these types of connections help establish the English language arts classroom as a safe place where students can reflect on and process the complicated world issues that face them on a daily basis.

Connecting the Extend Stage to Remote Instruction

We English language arts teachers can utilize the features and attributes of remote instruction to create ways for our students to extend ideas in literature to the world around them. Since the extend stage calls for students to place themselves and their understanding of literature in larger contexts, it aligns perfectly with a great deal of online information to which students have access during remote instruction. We educators can create opportunities for students to research real-world events, issues, and movements (while identifying credible sources) and connect the key aspects of those events, issues, and movements to important topics and issues in the literature they've read. For example, students can connect contemporary cultural and political issues with the sociopolitical context in a particular novel and compare the way individuals today work for change to the ways characters in texts attempt to bring about change to the communities in which they live. Through these kinds of activities, students can reflect, explore, and research issues that matter to them while considering the ways that literature provides ways for readers to consider not only the events and issues in a text but also important events in issues in the world around us.

Why Is It Important?

While there have certainly been many changes made to teaching and learning during the COVID-19 era and the corresponding increase in remote teaching and learning, one aspect of English language arts instruction that we believe should continue is the thought-provoking and multifaceted literature instruction presented by Milner et al. (2012). By providing students with opportunities to enter texts, explore key aspects, and extend their understandings, we can ensure that students in remote contexts can still engage in high-quality literature instruction.

The benefits of strong literature instruction are significant and numerous; the National Council of Teachers of English and the International Reading Association's (1996) Standards for the English Language Arts call for students to read "a wide range of literature from many periods in many genres to build an understanding of the many dimensions (e.g., philosophical, ethical, aesthetic) of human experience" and "a wide range of print and non-print texts to build an understanding of texts, of themselves, and of the cultures of the United States and the world." These statements illustrate the personal, academic, and societal benefits associated with effective literature instruction. By creating instructional opportunities for our students to meaningfully engage with a variety of texts and have engaging, meaningful, and multifaceted experiences with those works, we can provide them with instruction that will benefit them in a variety of ways throughout their lives. Conducting this type of literature instruction in the context of remote learning has challenging aspects, but we strongly believe that effective instruction using the practices and ideas discussed in this chapter is valuable and worth the time and effort.

Now, let's take a look at an example of Jennifer's work with the students in her middle school English class as she engages her students in remote literature instruction.

Instructional Snapshot: An Example From Jennifer's Work

The beloved short story "The Tell-Tale Heart" by Edgar Allen Poe is an engaging, fast-paced text that students love to read. It keeps students interested, allowing them to analyze the text and make inferences throughout the text. The tone and mood of the text shift as the plot builds, making it a perfect text to model mood and tone.

This lesson was taught over two days, with students activating their prior knowledge and entering the exploring stage on the first day. On the second day, students completed the exploring stage and went on to extend their knowledge. On the first day, I reviewed mood and tone using Google Slides and Pear Deck. Students often struggle with identifying the difference between the two, so a mini-lesson is appreciated prior to practicing the skills. We broke down what the difference between mood and tone is and how to identify the two in writing and practiced using pieces of a model text. Then, students entered the explore stage by being assigned a quick write with the prompt: "Would you spend the night in a graveyard for $1000? Why or why not?"

The goal of students' answering this prompt prior to reading is to allow them to write their personal feelings toward something dark prior to beginning the text. Once students finished their responses, they were asked to reflect on their writing. The following questions were given: How do you feel when you read your work? How did you feel writing it? What kind of verbs or adjectives did you use? Do your words tell the reader you are scared, excited, or nervous?

The next day, we began reading "The Tell-Tale Heart." Each student had a copy of the story and followed along as it was read to them. Students were given the instructions to identify the mood and tone of the story and look for key examples. As we read, students sent their analyses in the Zoom chat. As the story progressed, I hinted to the group that the mood and the tone of the story change toward the end. The goal was for the students to be able to identify the shift in word choice the narrator uses as he attempts to portray himself as a sane man.

At the conclusion of the text, we reviewed our observations together and confirmed the tone and the mood of the text. Then, students were assigned a Google Doc and asked to identify the mood and the tone of a news article of their choosing. Their Doc had a list of articles they could choose from to analyze, ranging from opinion pieces to sports news to politics. Students were asked to pull five sentences that support their claims of tone and mood, with gifted and honors students being challenged with ten. After completing their analysis, students were invited to present their findings, sharing their screen via Zoom and showcasing their claims and evidence.

Key Recommendations

In this section, we discuss key recommendations to keep in mind when engaging your students in remote literature instruction. These suggestions are designed to help you implement important and beneficial practices of literature instruction in the context of remote learning. They are constructed with Milner et al. (2012) ideas of enter, explore, and extend in mind, providing insights into how to adapt these concepts to remote instruction:

- Prior to reading, provide students with engaging opportunities to reflect on key issues in a text.
- While students read, create opportunities for them to make personal connections to a text.
- Design ways for students to engage in collaborative work about the texts they read.
- Use the features of remote learning to conduct mini-lessons and conferences for students as they construct their individual analyses of literary texts.
- Use the tools of remote learning to help students extend their knowledge of texts in meaningful ways.

By incorporating these suggestions, you'll provide your students with multilayered, engaging, and thought-provoking literature instruction that helps them explore literary works in depth while also maximizing the features of remote teaching and learning. Now, we explore these recommendations in more depth, describing their attributes and ways to put them into action in remote contexts.

Recommendation One: Prior to Reading, Provide Students With Engaging Opportunities to Reflect on Key Issues in a Text

To begin the process of remote literature instruction, we recommend providing students with ways to reflect on key issues in the literary work they will be reading. These activities, which activate students' prior knowledge and create accessible points of entry that allow them to reflect on key concepts in a text, are well suited for remote learning. Through remote learning, students can share their initial responses on and connections to key themes in a text in a variety of ways, such as chat features, breakout groups, and longer written responses. Students can even use all these remote learning features when reflecting on the same issue. For example, if students are reading a book with the theme of "Challenging Society's Expectations," they might first share their initial thoughts on that concept in the chat box. Then, if technology allows, they could further elaborate on those opening responses by discussing the ideas with peers in breakout groups. Sharing these ideas with peers and further elaborating on them can help students develop their insights even more, which will help them prepare even more to consider the concept in the text they read. Finally, students use the ideas, connections, and insights they've generated through this process to craft longer written responses through Google Docs, discussion board posts, or other remote learning tools that align with more detailed and developed responses.

This series of learning activities can be adapted and implemented in a variety of ways based on particular instructional modalities and learning resources you have available. While some specific components may differ for a range of reasons, we encourage you to use the tools of remote learning to provide your students with a variety of ways to consider and reflect on key issues in a text before reading it. The chart depicted in Figure 4.1 is one that Sean has used when helping teachers design learning activities based on students reflecting on key issues in texts before reading those works. This chart, which is meant to be a tool to guide your instructional planning, asks you to identify the text you're teaching, a key issue in the text, why you believe understanding that issue is important to students' experiences with the text, and some activities you'll use to help students engage with that issue. You

The Text You're Teaching	A Key Issue in the Text	Why Understanding This Issue Will Benefit Students	Some Activities You'll Use to Help Students Engage With This Issue

Figure 4.1 Key Issues Planning Chart

can use this chart repeatedly as you identify key issues and plan learning activities associated with various texts you teach.

Recommendation Two: While Students Read, Create Opportunities for Them to Make Personal Connections to a Text

After students have used the tools and features of remote learning to activate their prior knowledge about key themes and issues in a work of literature, we recommend focusing on students' during-reading experiences. An especially effective way to create meaningful reading experiences for students is to create opportunities for them to make personal connections to a text while reading. This practice is informed by Louise Rosenblatt's (1968), seminal piece *Literature as Exploration*, in which she describes the individualized process that readers experience when making sense of a text. According to Rosenblatt, texts do not have meaning on their own—the meaning of a piece for an individual reader is created through that reader's experience interacting with the text. These interactions can be informed by the personal connections we readers make when reading a text, highlighting the individualized nature of reading.

We feel that these individualized responses to literature are especially important during remote learning, as they help engage and validate students in a situation when learning can be especially difficult for some students. There are a range of ways to facilitate students' personal connections to texts while they read. Similar to the prereading tactics discussed in the previous recommendation, we suggest utilizing a range of remote learning tools that align with the specific types of connections students are being asked to make. For example, students might make shorter, more immediate connections in a chat box comment and share longer, more developed responses in a breakout group, on a Google Doc, or on a discussion board. These remote learning tools provide a variety of ways for students to make personal connections to the literature they read, which helps create individualized and meaningful reading experiences for them.

Recommendation Three: Design Ways for Students to Engage in Collaborative Work About the Texts They Read

While students continue to explore key ideas in literary works and develop their interpretations, we encourage you to use the features of remote learning to construct opportunities for them to engage in collaborative work focused on their responses and insights into the text. As we discussed earlier in this chapter in the "Connecting the Explore Stage to Remote Instruction," there are a variety of methods we teachers can incorporate for engaging students in collaborative remote literary analysis.

Regarding this variety of methods, we suggest that teachers do two things: (1) provide students with a range of collaboration activities and methods and (2) purposefully align each collaboration activity with its intended instructional goal. Giving students a range of remote ways to collaborate about the texts they read is beneficial because it helps facilitate their engagement in virtual learning. For example, if students collaborate in pairs in some instances, larger groups (such as those of four or five students) in other situations, and with the entire class in other situations, students can be increasingly engaged in their remote literature instruction than if every class discussion and collaboration followed the same format. In addition, varying the collaboration methods helps us as teachers align the activities we've constructed for our students with desired learning objectives. For example, if the goal of a collaboration is for students to share initial responses and reactions to a piece, they can offer insights verbally, write them in the chat box, or discuss them in Zoom breakout rooms. By contrast, if students are working together to create longer and more developed collaborative projects, such as group analyses of key themes, ideas, or characters, we suggest tools such as Google Docs and Google Slides that will create opportunities for them to work together over time and align with the features of larger-scale written pieces and presentations. (The collaboration ideas discussed in Chapter 2 provide additional information about ways to engage students in meaningful interaction using tools of remote learning.)

Recommendation Four: Use the Features of Remote Learning to Conduct Mini-Lessons and Conferences for Students as They Construct Their Individual Analyses of Literary Texts

We feel that an important aspect of effective literature instruction is the opportunity for students to share their own analyses of key concepts and issues in the texts they read. There are a variety of ways for students to construct works that convey their analyses: they might create essays that identify and explain important themes, construct creative applications of knowledge such as pieces that describe an important scene from another characters' perspective or discuss a new ending to the piece, or craft intertextual analyses such as written works that compare a key concept or issue in a book to another text a student has read.

No matter the specific form a literary analysis might take, a challenge for educators is how to best support students' work on these projects (and others like them) in the context of remote learning. To help students do this, we recommend using the features of remote learning to create mini-lessons and hold conferences with them as they work on these projects. In these remote mini-lessons, we recommend talking with students about the analytical strategies and other key insights they'll use in order to successfully complete their projects. Each mini-lesson can identify an aspect of literary analysis and discuss ways to apply that analytical component to the work students are creating at the time. These mini-lessons can be shared with students in real time through remote instruction and recorded for students to access later (and for students who were unable to participate in a real-time session to view when they're able). After conducting these mini-lessons, we suggest devoting instructional time to students working on their literary analyses and holding one-on-one writing conferences with them as they do so. As discussed in Chapter 3, these writing conferences can take a range of forms depending on specific technological availability, such as individual meetings through a Zoom-like platform and text-based exchanges via Google Docs. As explained in Chapter 3, regardless of the specific conference features, we recommend keeping a record of the conversation to help track student progress and development. (The writing conference graphic organizer depicted in Figure 3.2 will help you do this.)

Recommendation Five: Use the Tools of Remote Learning to Help Students Extend Their Knowledge of Texts in Meaningful Ways

The tools of remote learning can play important roles in instruction that helps students extend their knowledge of texts in meaningful and thought-provoking ways. There are key ways we suggest using remote learning tools during the "extend stage": (1) use the features of remote learning to facilitate students' abilities to make connections between a literary text and world issues and (2) utilizing remote learning technology to create authentic ways for students to share their insights. Each of these practices utilizes the features of remote learning in meaningful and relevant ways that help students connect ideas in a work of literature with social, cultural, and political ideas of their choice that are relevant and meaningful to them.

To achieve the first recommendation of using remote learning to facilitate students' abilities to make connections between a literary text and world issues, we recommend creating opportunities for students to conduct research on issues that they identified in the text and are relevant to them. To do this, students can identify and reflect on key ideas, issues, and concepts that they noticed in a literary work and then research world events that are also representative of these ideas. While students work on these extension activities, we teachers can support them by conducting mini-lessons about research-related topics, such as finding credible sources, identifying key points, and synthesizing information. We can then confer and check in with them as they do this, noting their progress and providing individualized research and writing suggestions.

Regarding the second recommendation, utilizing remote learning technology to create authentic ways for students to share their insights, we encourage you to look for ways that students can use digital resources to write for audiences that go beyond the teacher. For students to share their works with classmates, they can post their extension activities and connections to a class-wide discussion board on a learning management system such as Google Classroom or Canvas. You could also create opportunities for students to share their work with authentic audiences beyond the school by asking them to consider posting their works to a school or class website that can be read by others in and outside of the school. These opportunities for students to share their insights with others have the potential to increase motivation and relevance (Ruday, 2016) and are closely aligned with the digital tools featured in many forms of remote learning.

Adapting for a Range of Modalities

An important topic to consider in a discussion of remote literature instruction is the varying modalities in which remote teaching takes place and the ways to best adapt the best practices of remote literature instruction to these modalities. With this variation in mind, this section describes ideas to consider when implementing this chapter's insights on remote literature instruction across a range of modalities. In it, we describe insights to consider when implementing the chapter's points about effective literature instruction in a range of modes: entirely remote instruction (in which instruction is completely virtual), hybrid instruction (in which students are physically present in the classroom some days and engage through virtual learning other days), and hyflex instruction (in which some students are physically present in the classroom and other students join at the same time virtually). The modality adaptations discussed here are designed to provide you with additional support and recommendations as you engage your students in meaningful and thought-provoking literature instruction.

Instructional Modality	Key Suggestions to Consider
Entirely remote	Teaching literature in an entirely remote way lends itself to the use of a range of technological tools and resources that we teachers can use when helping our students engage with, explore, and extend their knowledge of literature. However, just because there are a variety of tools available does not mean that we should necessarily use every single one. We recommend that you reflect on the technological resources with which you and your students are comfortable and that best align with the instructional goals associated with each activity. For example, the technological tools and innovations used when students make initial

Instructional Modality	Key Suggestions to Consider
	connections to key issues in a text or develop personal connections to concepts in the book will differ from those you use when you conduct mini-lessons on key aspects of literary analyses or communicate with students one-on-one about their writing. We encourage you to think first about the learning goal of each activity and then select the technological tool that you feel will best help you and your students work together to achieve that goal.
Hybrid	We feel that the most effective hybrid literature instruction is based on the idea that planning decisions should correspond with the ways students are participating in class on particular days. Since students engaging in hybrid instruction participate in virtual learning on some days and in-person classes on others, we recommend that you reflect on which instructional practices and technological tools would work best with in-person instruction and which ones work best for online learning. When applying this idea specifically to literature instruction, you might consider how students are participating on a particular day (either in person or virtually) and how to best facilitate student learning in that form of participation. For example, if your students are learning in person on a day when they are making personal connections to a text they read, you can construct activities that align with in-person interactions, such as students writing ideas in a response journal and then verbally sharing them with others in the classroom. Then, if students are learning virtually on another day, you can select activities that are more aligned with virtual participation. For instance, if students are collaboratively discussing ideas in a literary text on a virtual learning day, you can create opportunities for them to discuss key insights using Zoom breakout rooms, Google Docs, online discussion boards, or other similar tools.

Instructional Modality	Key Suggestions to Consider
Hyflex	The best hyflex literature instruction is designed in ways that incorporate the components of this multifaceted modality, which calls for some students to join the class online at the same time others are present in person. When teaching literature in a hyflex way, we recommend incorporating both groups simultaneously. For example, if students are working collaboratively to share their interpretations of a text, all students could interact using the same Google Doc or discussion board whether they are joining the class virtually or in person. This would allow all students to participate and share their responses in a common way. If you are explaining a key concept or conducting a mini-lesson about an important aspect of a literary analysis, we suggest identifying ways that will allow for all students to access the information at the same time, such as broadcasting the explanation on Zoom or a similar platform for students joining virtually while also sharing it with the in-person students. You could also record the explanation so that students joining online can be able to access it in the event of technical challenges that might limit their abilities to livestream the content.

5

Culturally Relevant and Sustaining Teaching and Learning in Remote Contexts

In this chapter, we reflect on the best practices for implementing culturally relevant (Ladson-Billings, 1995) and culturally sustaining pedagogy (Paris, 2012) in remote English language arts instruction. As we discuss in this chapter, culturally relevant and culturally sustaining instructional practices are essential to all English language arts instruction and can be effectively utilized in remote learning to provide teaching and learning activities that center students' identities and experiences. Through the information in this chapter, we discuss key characteristics of culturally relevant and sustaining teaching and provide suggestions to consider when putting these ideas into action in remote instruction. First, we explore important aspects of culturally relevant and sustaining pedagogy, focusing on how it can be connected to remote English language arts instruction. Then we reflect on why it's so important to implement culturally relevant and sustaining instruction in remote contexts. We follow this information with an instructional snapshot section that provides an example of Jennifer's work with her middle school students. Then we share key recommendations for teachers to consider when putting culturally relevant and sustaining English language arts instruction in action. Finally, we discuss how the ideas in this chapter can be implemented in a range of modalities.

What Are the Key Aspects of Remote Culturally Relevant and Sustaining English Instruction?

Let's begin our exploration of remote culturally relevant and sustaining English instruction by considering the fundamental components of these concepts. In her seminal article "But That's Just Good Teaching! The Case for Culturally Relevant Pedagogy," Gloria Ladson-Billings (1995) explains that

> [c]ulturally relevant pedagogy rests on three criteria or propositions: (a) Students must experience academic success; (b) students must develop and/or maintain cultural competence; and (c) students must develop a critical consciousness through which they challenge the status quo of the current social order.
>
> (p. 160)

Instructional practices that incorporate these three criteria can take a number of forms. Ladson-Billings shares that the teachers she studied who implemented culturally relevant teaching not only used a variety of strategies and methods but also had a number of important aspects in common: they felt invested in the communities in which they taught, strongly believed that all students could succeed, and centered students in the curriculum through "fluid and equitable" relationships that created space for students to share their ideas and perspectives in the classroom (p. 163).

Django Paris, in his (2012) piece "Culturally Sustaining Pedagogy: A Needed Change in Stance, Terminology, and Practice," builds off Ladson-Billings's (1995) work and suggests shifting the phrasing and practice from "culturally relevant" to "culturally sustaining," asserting that pedagogy that effectively centers students will work toward sustaining their cultures and identities:

> The term culturally sustaining requires that our pedagogies be more than responsive of or relevant to the cultural experiences and practices of young people—it requires that they support young people in sustaining the cultural and linguistic competence of their communities while simultaneously offering access to dominant cultural competence.
>
> (p. 95)

Instruction that is culturally relevant and culturally sustaining is characterized by instructional practices that value and center students' identities, which helps create opportunities for students' academic success. We can make our classroom culturally sustaining by providing students with opportunities to make authentic connections between academic concepts they learn in school and aspects of their out-of-school lives. In English instruction, students can apply their knowledge of reading strategies, writing tactics, and word-study components to texts with which they authentically interact in their cultures, communities, and lived experiences.

We've found that the features of remote English instruction and culturally sustaining pedagogies align very well: students can connect key concepts, strategies, and ideas they learn about in their instruction to texts with which they authentically interact in their out-of-school lives. For example, in an instructional sequence focused on figurative language, a teacher can use the principles of culturally relevant and sustaining pedagogy to center students' identities and experiences by constructing opportunities for students to apply this concept to texts they encounter in authentic contexts. In this type of instruction, the teacher could begin by sharing a mini-lesson on figurative language and providing them with a range of examples of its use. After that, the students could reflect on the importance of figurative language and the reasons authors use it in their works. After that, students can identify examples of figurative language they encounter in their out-of-school lives and share them with their classmates using the tools of remote learning. Instructional practices such as this center students' unique experiences and prioritize the forms of literacy with which they engage in out-of-school environments (Duncan-Andrade & Morrell, 2005). While this specific example addresses figurative language, we look in this chapter at a variety of specific topics and concepts that can be meaningfully examined using culturally relevant and culturally sustaining pedagogy.

Why Is It Important?

As Ladson-Billings (1995) and Paris (2012) describe, culturally relevant and culturally sustaining pedagogy is essential to creating equitable learning experiences for students. Similarly, Duncan-Andrade and Morrell (2005) advocate for instructional practices that facilitate authentic connections to students' lives. These ideas are integral to equity-minded instruction in all contexts. Related specifically to remote English language arts instruction, the features and principles of culturally relevant and sustaining pedagogy are essential concepts for teachers to consider when organizing remote learning experiences for their students. Since culturally relevant and sustaining pedagogy centers students in the curriculum and values their cultures and identities in the ways that Ladson-Billings (1995) and Paris (2012) describe, it presents a natural connection to the aspects and affordances of remote learning, in which students are not bound by the traditional structures and spaces of school in ways they previously were. In traditional schooling, students leave their homes to enter a distinct physical place. By contrast, in remote learning, students typically are engaging in at least some of their academic work from their homes. (The specific amount of time students spend at home depends on details such as whether they are learning entirely online or in hybrid or hyflex formats.)

We feel that the opportunities remote learning presents for students to learn outside of school also creates outstanding connections to culturally relevant and sustaining pedagogy: because students are physically in their communities while they learn, we as educators can create additional opportunities for students' communities and their associated interests, cultures, and backgrounds to incorporate into our instruction. Jamila Lyiscott (2019) calls for educators to create space for students by recognizing and valuing their realities, perspectives, and identities. Through remote learning, we can create these spaces and opportunities by asking students to use the features of remote instruction to facilitate authentic connections between texts with which students interact in their out-of-school lives and the concepts they study in school.

Now, let's take a look at an example of Jennifer's work with the students in her middle school English class as she applies ideas of culturally relevant and sustaining pedagogy to her remote instruction.

Instructional Snapshot: An Example From Jennifer's Work

During remote instruction, keeping students involved in novel studies has been more difficult. One way to combat this has been creating journals using Google Slides. A teacher within my professional learning community came up with the idea and created Slides that broke down plot, characters, and conflict. It worked well with students and for us teachers as well to monitor progress and offer feedback.

As the state test grew near and we began increasing our focus on grammar, I chose to use the interactive journals via Slides again. I created the journals to focus specifically on grammatical concepts, and they contained notes, practice items, examples in our novel, and opportunities to make real-world connections. We reviewed capitalization, comma usage, prepositional phrases, verb tense consistency, comparative and superlative degrees, and quotation marks with dialogue and direct quotes. These grammatical concepts were difficult for my students to comprehend, so having one project that reviewed and spiraled these concepts in one was beneficial.

The Slides were split by concept, beginning with notes and sentences to practice with in isolation. Then, the Slides offered examples from the novel so that students may see the concepts used in a text. Students then proceeded to the next section, in which they pulled examples of the grammatical concept being studied from songs, movies, other books, articles, or even social media posts.

This project allowed students to practice important grammatical concepts in isolation, see them in a mentor text, and then identify them in texts all around them. This is a key tool in keeping students engaged in their learning and showing them how important their learning is to their everyday lives.

Key Recommendations

In this section, we share and describe important recommendations for implementing culturally relevant and sustaining pedagogy in remote English instruction. These suggestions are designed to help you incorporate essential aspects of Ladson-Billings's (1995) and Paris's (2012) concepts of culturally relevant and sustaining pedagogy in your English instruction while also considering the aspects of and opportunities associated with remote learning. The recommendations are designed to center students' authentic experiences and perspectives in remote language arts instruction, creating the "fluid and equitable" instruction that Ladson-Billings (1995, p. 163) describes and the space for students' unique perspectives and identities discussed by Lyiscott (2019).

- Create video mini-lessons that describe key literacy strategies and provide examples of their authentic, real-world uses.
- Use the tools of remote learning to help students reflect on the importance of authentically used literacy strategies.
- Ask students to find real-world examples of literacy strategies and concepts and consider their significance.
- Provide students with remote opportunities to share the real-world examples they identified and analyzed.

Now, we examine these suggestions in more detail, considering their key features, ways to put them into action, and the ways they center students' individual backgrounds in culturally relevant and sustaining ways.

Recommendation One: Create Video Mini-Lessons That Describe Key Literacy Strategies and Provide Examples of Their Authentic, Real-World Uses

We recommend beginning this instructional process by creating video mini-lessons for students that not only describe key literacy strategies and concepts but also provide examples of the authentic, real-world uses of these concepts. This opening step prepares students for the work they will do as they progress through this sequence by introducing the academic topic on which they will focus and illustrating some ways that the concept looks in authentic situations. We educators can use this activity to introduce and discuss any literacy strategy. Figure 5.1 depicts some literacy-related concepts and strategies that teachers can describe and connect to authentic, real-world applications and uses.

When constructing a video mini-lesson on a literacy strategy and its authentic uses, we recommend first discussing the concept's essential features by sharing its definition and a few examples related to the students' previous academic work. For example, when discussing the idea of strong verbs, we can talk with students about the attributes of this concept and relate it to examples of strong verbs in a text that students have read that school year. After that, we can connect this concept to authentic, real-world usage by sharing with students examples of strong verbs in a text with which you engage outside of school. For instance, when conducting a mini-lesson on this topic, Sean, an avid sports fan, talked with students about the strong verbs he encounters when watching, listening to, and reading about sports. By doing so, he provided students with examples of this concept he encountered in his out-of-school life. This practice provided a model of real-world application of this writing strategy and worked to show that the class was a place where out-of-school lives and real-world texts are valued. By presenting this

Writing	**Reading**	**Language study**
• Strong verbs • Specific nouns • Connotation-rich words • Engaging leads • Sensory detail	• Inferences • Connections • Analysis of mood • Predictions • Context clues	• Domain-specific vocabulary relevant to students' authentic experiences • Examples of word roots students encounter in their out-of-school lives

Figure 5.1 Examples of Literacy Concepts and Strategies

Note: While these are some examples of concepts that we feel can play important roles in effective English language arts instruction, we encourage you to select topics that relate to your students' specific needs and the relevant standards for your local context.

information to students through video mini-lessons, we can provide them with resources that they can access repeatedly and are aligned with both synchronous and asynchronous instruction. In addition, the connection between academic concepts and authentic uses that is central to this activity aligns with Ladson-Billings's (1995) statement that culturally relevant teaching must be used to facilitate students' academic success while also creating relevant and culturally affirming instruction.

Recommendation Two: Use the Tools of Remote Learning to Engage Students in Collaborative Analyses of the Importance of Authentically Used Literacy Strategies

Once you've shared with students video mini-lessons that describe and provide authentic examples of literacy strategies, we recommend using the tools of remote learning to create opportunities for students to collaboratively analyze authentically used literacy strategies. To do this, we suggest modeling for students what it looks like to analyze the importance of a literacy strategy used in an authentic, real-world context and then engaging them in collaborative analyses of the importance of that strategy to effective communication and understanding. We recommend beginning this activity by providing students with a video model analysis of a specific concept and then asking them to work collaboratively using remote learning tools to analyze the focal strategy.

For example, after Sean shared with students examples of strong verbs from broadcasts and articles about sports, he engaged them in a remote activity that asked students to think about why those strong verbs were important to the effectiveness of the works in which they were used. First, he modeled for students his analysis of how one of the strong verbs he identified in the previous activity was important to the effectiveness of the article in which it initially appeared, sharing his insights into why the sportswriter used that verb and how the passage would be different if the author didn't use it. After that, he provided students other examples from the video mini-lesson discussed in step one of this process and asked them to work together in breakout rooms to analyze these examples. Each group analyzed a strong verb example together and shared its thoughts on a Google Slide, providing information about why the author chose to use the concept, its importance to the context in which it was used, and how the piece would be different if it wasn't used.

By engaging in this activity, students were able to think about and develop metacognitive understandings of how literacy concepts such as this one are used in authentic ways. While this specific example focuses on strong verbs in sportswriting, this collaborative remote analysis can be applied to all types of real-world applications of literacy strategies. For example, a teacher can model for students how reading strategies such as making connections and constructing inferences can be applied to texts we read in authentic situations as well as how language study concepts such as identifying word roots and using those roots to interpret word meanings. Regardless of the specific concept being analyzed, students can use remote learning features to engage in collaborative analyses of authentic uses of literacy concepts, which can help them understand how these concepts are used in out-of-school contexts: a skill that they will further develop in the next step of this instructional process.

Recommendation Three: Ask Students to Find Real-World Examples of Literacy Strategies and Concepts and Consider Their Significance

At this stage in the instructional process, students take on increased responsibility and ownership for their learning. In it, students look for authentic, real-world texts that contain or align with the literacy strategy or concept they have been learning about throughout the instructional process. The text that students choose to analyze can be from their lives in any authentic context. By asking students to consider real-world texts with these literacy strategies and concepts in mind, we educators can center students in the curriculum by creating opportunities for them to see connections between these concepts and their everyday lives. This practice aligns with Paris's (2012) statement that culturally sustaining pedagogy privileges cultural and linguistic aspects of students' communities.

When students do this, we teachers ask them to identify examples of a focal concept in any text that represents their authentic interests, experiences, cultures, and/or identities and then reflect on the importance of that concept to the text in which it is located. By doing this, students follow the same cognitive process demonstrated in the first two steps of this instructional process but do so in ways that provide them with more ownership and agency. This activity creates space for students to incorporate into the classroom the texts and topics with which they authentically engage. As we construct these opportunities for students to look for these texts, it's important that we educators value a wide range of texts with which students interact. Emily Machado (2017) asserts that "culturally sustaining pedagogy also encourages us to consider the term 'culture' in a broader sense, including concepts such as popular, youth, and local culture alongside those associated with ethnicity" (para. 2) and identifies a range of ways she and her colleagues have seen students conceptualize culture, such as "Chicago culture, culinary culture, digital culture, and more" (para. 6). By expressing to students that the texts they analyze can take a wide range of forms and focuses, we can work toward constructing student-centered, relevant, and equitable instruction.

This activity connects very well to the features of remote learning: since remote instruction involves students spending more time in their homes and communities and less in the physical environment of school, it facilitates authentic opportunities for students to look at the world around them for examples of focal literacy strategies. For example, students who are focusing on strong verbs in the world around them can consider a range of ways they see, hear, and engage with this concept on an everyday basis in their authentic lives. While students work on this activity, we recommend holding one-on-one conferences with them utilizing remote learning tools. If technology allows, you can hold these conferences with students using individual Zoom breakout rooms. Alternately, students can record their identifications and analyses on Google Docs and you can provide them with questions and suggestions via comments on the documents.

Recommendation Four: Provide Students With Remote Opportunities to Share the Real-World Examples They Identified and Analyzed

Now that students have explored examples of literacy concepts in authentic, real-world texts, it's time for the final step of this instructional process. At this stage, we teachers provide students with remote opportunities to use the features of distance learning in order to share the culturally relevant examples they identified and analyzed. These opportunities to share can take a range of forms. Depending on technological capabilities and available resources, students could create prerecorded presentations that they upload for others to view or they could share synchronous presentations that they share with classmates in real time. However, students can also share their insights in ways they go beyond presentations: they can also create infographics or one-pagers that describe the authentic examples of literacy concepts they identified and analyzed. Whether students give presentations or create documents (or both!) remotely to share their insights, we recommend ensuring that classmates have opportunities to use the tools of remote learning to comment on what they learned from one another's works. Some great benefits of this activity are how much students can learn about their classmates' identities and how students can share their authentic perspectives with one another.

No matter what specific format you ask students to use when sharing their identifications and analysis (or if you provide them with a range of possible options to use when doing so), an important feature of this stage of the instructional process is that it centers students' unique ideas, insights, and positionalities. By constructing opportunities for students to share real-world connections that value their individual identities, interests, and experiences, we educators are conveying to students that we value the cultures with which our students identify and are committed to creating space in their curriculum for them to share authentic applications of literacy concepts. By doing so, we construct opportunities for students to express their identities and voices (Lyiscott, 2019) and incorporate key principles of culturally relevant (Ladson-Billings, 1995) and culturally sustaining pedagogy (Paris, 2012) in our remote English instruction.

Adapting for a Range of Modalities

In this section, we provide ideas to consider when putting this chapter's insights into action in the varying modalities of remote English instruction. While the essential attributes of culturally relevant and sustaining pedagogy can be enacted in all modalities, certain aspects of its implementation will vary based on the ways the students are able to interact with the teacher and with one another. Because of this, we share here some ideas to consider when implementing this chapter's ideas about culturally relevant and sustaining English instruction in a range of modes: entirely remote instruction (in which instruction is completely virtual), hybrid instruction (in which students are physically present in the classroom some days and engage through virtual learning other days), and hyflex instruction (in which some students are physically present in the classroom and other students join at the same time virtually). The modality adaptations discussed here are designed to provide you with additional support and recommendations as you implement the ideas discussed in this chapter in your instruction.

Instructional Modality	Key Suggestions to Consider
Entirely remote	When engaging students in entirely remote English instruction that facilitates authentic connections to their out-of-school lives and interests, you can use a variety of resources and technological tools for students to collaborate, learn, and share. We recommend keeping in mind how each tool aligns with the particular activity in which you are engaging your students. For example, a video mini-lesson you deliver will align with different technological resources than a collaborative activity. Also, when teaching students remotely, we encourage you to help them capitalize on the fact that they are learning in their homes and communities, which facilitates the kinds of connections between literacy concepts and authentic, real-world texts with which students interact.
Hybrid	An important principle to consider when planning hybrid instruction is that the instructional tools used should align with whether students are learning in person or online. Since students learning in hybrid ways participate in virtual instruction on some days and in-person classes on others, we encourage you to think about how the aspects of culturally relevant and pedagogy align with the specific features of virtual and in-person learning. For instance, if students are working virtually on a day they are working to identify and analyze examples of literacy concepts in their out-of-school lives, you can use the features and attributes of virtual learning to guide them as they do this analysis. Similarly, if students are meeting in person on days they share the authentic examples they found and their analyses of those examples, you'll want to structure the sharing activities in ways that correspond with in-person interaction.

Instructional Modality	Key Suggestions to Consider
Hyflex	Because hyflex teaching involves some students being physically in the classroom at the same time others join the class online, we recommend thinking about ways that allow both groups to participate in learning activities as effectively as possible. For example, if some students are present in the classroom on a day when students are collaboratively analyzing the importance of a literacy concept to an authentic text and others are joining virtually at the same time, we suggest using technological tools such as Google Slides and Google Docs that allow for students to collaborate and share ideas regardless of their physical location at the time. When students join the class virtually, they can also share authentic examples of real-world texts around them with all the other students in the class, which can further illustrate what real-world applications of concepts can look like and build a learning community that understands and values culturally relevant and sustaining English instruction.

6

The Role of Inquiry in Remote Teaching and Learning

In this chapter, we explore the role of inquiry-based teaching and learning in remote English language arts instruction. As we discuss in this chapter, inquiry-based English language arts instruction is a pedagogical framework that not only privileges students' curiosities and interests (Ruday & Caprino, 2021) but also aligns well with the features of remote learning. In this chapter, we describe what inquiry-based English language arts instruction is and share ideas to consider when implementing this instructional approach remotely. First, we examine key aspects of effective inquiry-based remote English instruction, which we follow by exploring the importance of this pedagogical framework to effective teaching in remote contexts. After that, we look at an instructional snapshot section that provides an example of Jennifer's work with her middle school students. Then, we share recommendations for teachers to consider when putting inquiry-based remote English instruction into action. Finally, we discuss how the ideas in this chapter can be implemented in a range of modalities.

What Are the Key Aspects of Inquiry-Based Remote English Instruction?

Inquiry-based pedagogy is a form of teaching and learning that centers on thought-provoking, big-picture essential questions that students investigate (McTighe & Wiggins, 2013). An essential question is defined as "a question that lies at the heart of a subject or a curriculum (as opposed to either being trivial or leading), and promotes inquiry and uncoverage of a subject" (Wiggins & McTighe, 2005, p. 342). A strong essential question, according to McTighe and Wiggins (2013, p. 3), should possess all or most of these seven attributes:

- is open-ended;
- is thought-provoking;
- calls for higher-order thinking;
- points toward important, transferable ideas;
- raises additional questions and sparks further inquiry;
- requires support and justification, not just an answer;
- and recurs over time, or can be revisited frequently.

By utilizing essential questions, we English language arts teachers can incorporate the features and benefits of inquiry-based learning in our English instruction. While essential questions can be applied to a range of subjects, they are especially useful and beneficial in English language arts because of the ways they provide opportunities for students to think about relevant and engaging issues that are present across the works with which they interact. The approach therefore "positions *authentic, real-world questions, not specific texts* at the center of your English curriculum" (Ruday & Caprino, 2021, p. 11). By engaging in inquiry-based English language arts instruction, students are able to engage with essential questions that facilitate authentic connections with their lives and real-world issues and can draw on their experiences interacting with a wide range of texts as they reflect on and construct their responses to those questions (Ruday & Caprino, 2021).

We feel that inquiry-based English language arts instruction is especially aligned with remote teaching and learning. The features of remote learning, such as the opportunities it provides for students to work independently and in self-directed ways, match up very well with the nature of inquiry-based learning. Since this instructional approach prioritizes students' unique experiences investigating questions and topics that have real-world connections, it lends itself to individualized explorations that can take place through a number of learning modalities and structures. Once students know the essential question they're investigating and have clear understandings of how to conduct an inquiry, they can work remotely on analyzing a range of texts that address that question. While students work on these inquiries remotely, we teachers can support them in a variety of ways. We can use the features of remote learning to provide students with guidance, such as sharing video mini-lessons on important ideas to keep in mind, giving feedback on their work through Google Docs, holding one-on-one conferences with them through Zoom, and constructing ways for students to offer virtual support to each other. Ultimately, once they've completed their inquiries, students can share the results of their investigations through remote presentation tools. Now, we consider why remote inquiry-based English language arts is important to effective remote teaching and learning.

Why Is It Important?

Inquiry-based learning can benefit students in a variety of ways: works such as Krebs and Zvi's (2015) *The Genius Hour Guidebook* and Juliani's (2015) *Inquiry and Innovation in the Classroom: Using 20% Time, Genius Hour, and PBL to Drive Student Success* discuss how inquiry-oriented experiences can maximize student engagement and achievement. These benefits are especially applicable to remote instruction, which presents significant challenges for teachers as they work to engage students and help them achieve academic goals: in a 2020 *New York Times* article titled "Students, Parents and Teachers Tell Their Stories of Remote Learning" by Amelia Nierenberg, students reported less motivation and lower academic performance during remote learning.

Inquiry-based instruction is of great importance to remote English language arts because the engagement and achievement it facilitates address the key challenges that students in Nierenberg's piece described. By providing students with opportunities to conduct multitextual inquiries that revolve around authentic, real-world essential questions, we can construct learning opportunities for our students that excite them about learning and help enhance academic achievement. Remote English language arts instruction is an especially apropos context for experiencing the benefits of inquiry-based learning since the use of essential questions is naturally linked with strong English language arts teaching and learning. When we pose essential questions and challenge our students to use a variety of texts in order to respond to those questions, we construct meaningful, relevant, and engaging learning opportunities for our students. By contrast, if we ask our students to read and analyze single, specific works without utilizing essential questions to help them consider important issues in those texts, it would be harder for students to engage in the authentic learning that inquiry-based instruction facilitates. When we construct opportunities for students to examine thought-provoking, engaging, and relevant questions that facilitate higher order thinking and require complex analysis (McTighe & Wiggins, 2013), we can help our students have engaging and motivating learning experiences in our remote English language arts classes.

Now, let's take a look at an example of Jennifer's work with the students in her middle school English class as she incorporates inquiry-based instruction.

Instructional Snapshot: An Example From Jennifer's Work

The Outsiders by S. E. Hinton is a novel that seems to stay with the times. And why is that? *The Outsiders* is a classic coming-of-age story that explores identity, trauma, socioeconomic status, stereotypes, and crime. The novel was released in 1967, and the problems the characters encounter are as applicable today as they were then. Students are able to relate to the characters and events, making real-world connections and personal anecdotes.

The unit begins with our class defining what inquiry is and how we can use literature to perform research. *The Outsiders* is introduced as our novel for the next few weeks, as well as "We Real Cool" by Gwendolyn Brooks; "Herd Behavior," a short essay written by CommonLit™; "Nothing Gold Can Stay" by Robert Frost; and Susan Hinton's 1967 short essay "Teen-Agers Are for Real." These texts will help students explore external factors on the making of one's identity.

We began with our unit's Google Slides assignment, which contains all questions, activities, and links additional texts for students to work through in this unit. Creating one set of Slides with all activities and resources within to be continuously worked on throughout the unit is helpful in keeping students focused, productive, and organized. The first few Slides list our unit's essential questions, with a slide following for students to list their raw responses prior to beginning the novel.

The overarching essential question for this unit is, "How can our community and environment affect our identity?" This question was broken down with the following:

1. What is identity? Are we born with our identities, or do we create them?
2. How can one's socioeconomic status affect their sense of identity?
3. Why do people change parts of themselves in order to fit in?

The first assignment in the Google Slides is for students to respond to these questions with their own opinions and ideas. Once that is complete, the class begins the novel. Guiding questions are listed in the Slides assignment for students to answer as they read, focusing on events that occurred in the chapter and asking for supporting details. Each chapters' questions are tailored to break down the essential questions and allow students to combine their comprehension of the text with their own opinions and knowledge of the real world. This is essential to ensuring students are reflecting on their reading and actively developing their own opinions and ideas in response to the unit's essential questions.

When students reach chapter 9 of *The Outsiders*, I share that our assessment for this unit will be done in the form of a project. I present a model in which

I used the same texts to answer the essential question, "Why is it important to belong?" I presented my answer to the question via Zoom, where I shared my slideshow and narrated it. From there, students began working on their own projects. Students could choose to also create a slideshow and narrate it, simply create a slideshow, create a poster or brochure, or record a Flipgrid and talk through their findings.

As we continue reading and finish *The Outsiders*, students are given designated times to work on their projects in class. Part of their assessment grade is to check in with me to get an update on their progress and to hear any troubles that are being had. The goal of this project is for students to work through the texts and reflect on their findings until they feel they have an answer that best reflects the truth to the essential question, "How can our community and environment affect our identity?"

Key Recommendations

Now, we share important suggestions to consider when incorporating inquiry-based learning in your remote English language arts instruction. These recommendations are designed to help you engage and support your students in ways that embody the best practices of inquiry-based teaching and learning while applying this approach to remote contexts. By implementing these suggestions in your instruction, you'll help your students learn using essential questions (Wiggins & McTighe, 2005; McTighe & Wiggins, 2013) and achieve the motivation and engagements benefits of inquiry-based learning (Krebs & Zvi, 2015; Juliani, 2015), which are especially aligned with English language arts instruction (Ruday & Caprino, 2021) and are particularly important to the context of remote teaching and learning, in which many students struggle with feeling motivated for and engaged in school (Nierenberg, 2020).

Our four recommendations for implementing inquiry-based remote English language arts instruction are as follows:

- Share video mini-lessons that convey the fundamental components of inquiry.
- Use the features of remote learning to help students respond to the texts they read and connect those texts to the inquiry's essential question.
- Provide remote support for students as they synthesize their responses to the unit's essential question.
- Create ways for students to remotely share the results of their inquiries and analyses.

Now, let's think in more detail about these recommendations, specific ways to put them into action, and why they represent effective remote inquiry-based English language arts instruction.

Recommendation One: Share Video Mini-Lessons That Convey the Fundamental Components of Inquiry

We recommend beginning the process of remote inquiry-based English language arts instruction by creating and sharing with students videos that convey key aspects of inquiry. Depending on the specific nature of your instructional delivery and your school's remote learning format, these could be prerecorded videos you share or live instruction you conduct. No matter which format your instruction takes, we recommend providing students with two short video mini-lessons. In the first one, we suggest talking about inquiry and essential questions in general, sharing with students the way inquiry involves using a variety of sources to answer one or more essential questions, talking with them about the features of essential questions, and providing them with some examples of inquiry. Then, in the next mini-lesson, we recommend describing the essential question students will investigate in the inquiry the class will conduct and the texts that will make up that inquiry. These brief, focused lessons will orient students to the essential aspects of inquiry-based English instruction and prepare them for the work they'll do throughout the unit as they interpret a variety of texts, synthesize their key ideas, and use the information in those texts to answer the unit's essential question.

Recommendation Two: Use the Features of Remote Learning to Help Students Respond to the Texts They Read and Connect Those Texts to the Inquiry's Essential Question

Now that students understand key aspects of inquiry-based English language arts learning, the next step is to engage them in this process by helping them respond to the texts they encounter in the inquiry. By constructing these responses, students can interpret the unit's texts and connect them to the essential question on which this learning process is focused. To maximize the effectiveness of doing so in remote learning, we recommend reflecting on the features of remote learning that you believe will best help students share their responses to the works they read in the inquiry. When constructing these activities, we recommend varying the remote learning tools based on the types of responses you want students to create. For example, as we've discussed in previous chapters, if students are sharing brief responses, such as initial reactions to a text's events or characters, they can do so using tools that facilitate those kinds of responses, such as a chat box comment. By contrast, when students compose longer, more developed responses, such as text-based inferences, connections to world events, or detailed discussions of a character's motivation, we recommend constructing response options that align with the time and space these responses would take, such as Google Docs, Zoom breakout group discussions, or online discussion boards.

Since inquiry-based English instruction is rooted in students' reflections on essential questions, the most effective remote reading responses in this context are those that gradually develop students' awareness of key issues in the texts and provide opportunities for them to connect their insights to the concepts that the essential question presents. While these specific responses can take a range of forms, the inquiry's essential questions can establish a common thread in the ways we ask our students to respond to the texts they encounter. By using the inquiry's essential question as a framework for student responses, we can prepare students for the next stage of this instructional process, in which students work to synthesize their insights about the essential question.

Recommendation Three: Provide Remote Support for Students as they Synthesize Their Responses to the Unit's Essential Question

After students remotely respond to the texts they read as part of this inquiry, the next step is for us as teachers to support them as they synthesize their understandings of those texts and use those insights to help them respond to the essential question. (Students will ultimately share the results of their inquiries and their corresponding analyses in the final step of this instructional process.) To help students synthesize their responses, we recommend providing a range of support opportunities designed to help them as they reflect on the texts they've read and how those texts combine to help them address the essential question. An initial step to help students synthesize their ideas is to provide them with a model of what this kind of analysis looks like. For example, when explaining to students how they'll synthesize their insights, you could share with them how you've done similar work by sharing with them a different essential question that you've investigated and describing how you used a range of texts to address this question. This can be done through the form of a video mini-lesson like those described in the initial step of this instructional sequence. By providing students with this information, you'll share with them in an accessible way what the synthesis process looks like and give them a framework that they can then apply to the essential question they're investigating.

After you've shared this model with students and discussed it with them, we recommend using remote learning tools to support students individually as they construct their own interpretations. Depending on the specific nature of your remote instruction, you could support students through one-on-one conferences in Zoom breakout rooms, feedback via Google Docs, recorded voice memos, or other methods of providing students with individualized responses. The best method of support to use is one that aligns with the features of your remote learning context and will be useful and accessible to your students. Regardless of the specific support tactic you utilize, we suggest sharing with students individualized feedback that focuses on the ways they are synthesizing the key ideas from the texts they've examined in ways that address the unit's essential question. As students craft their responses, it's important that they address the essential question in ways that represent their unique perspectives and that they develop their insights with specific evidence from the text. By using these remote learning tools, you can provide students with support as they create and fine-tune these responses and analyses.

Recommendation Four: Create Ways for Students to Remotely Share the Results of Their Inquiries and Analyses

In the final step of this instructional process, students remotely share the results of their inquiries by expressing how they've synthesized the texts they examined in the unit and used them to craft responses to the unit's essential question. These opportunities to share their insights can provide excellent learning experiences for students, as they not only get to share their own analyses and syntheses but also are able to learn from the ways that their classmates responded to the unit's essential questions. The similarities and differences between students' inquiry-based insights can provide excellent opportunities for students to reflect on common threads and to learn from the additional points and ideas their classmates made but they had not.

In order to create ways for students to share these results remotely, we recommend providing them with a range of options that align with the focus of the activity. Like with the out-of-school connections and applications described in Chapter 5, there are a variety of methods students can utilize as they share their inquiry responses. For example, students can construct recorded video presentations that convey their responses to the essential question and the ways the unit's text helped them reach that conclusion. These presentations can be shared synchronously if that aligns with your instructional delivery method or could be recorded and shared asynchronously. Alternately, students can create written responses, infographics, or one-pagers and share them with their classmates synchronously or asynchronously. No matter what kind of product students use to share their ideas and whether their works are shared synchronously or asynchronously, we recommend building in remote opportunities for students to comment on one another's inquiry results by providing compliments on their peers' insights, similarities to their own works, and ways their classmates' ideas helped them consider new ideas. These opportunities to share can emphasize the individualized nature of inquiry, call attention to commonalities, and build a collaborative remote learning community.

Adapting for a Range of Modalities

When implementing these ideas about remote inquiry-based English language arts instruction, it's important to consider the range of modalities in which remote learning can take place and make adaptations according to the form that aligns with the context in which you and your students are working. With that in mind, we share in this section ideas to consider when putting this chapter's key ideas about inquiry-based English language arts instruction in a variety of modalities: entirely remote instruction (in which instruction is completely virtual), hybrid instruction (in which students are physically present in the classroom some days and engage through virtual learning other days), and hyflex instruction (in which some students are physically present in the classroom and other students join at the same time virtually). These adaptation suggestions are designed to help you best align the principles of inquiry-based literature instruction with specific instructional modalities.

Instructional Modality	Key Suggestions to Consider
Entirely remote	When engaging students in inquiry-based instruction in an entirely remote modality, we recommend reflecting on the remote tools and resources available and selecting those that best align with specific activities. For example, when sharing information with students about the key aspects of inquiry-based learning and the features of essential questions, we suggest using video mini-lessons like those described in the chapter. By contrast, when supporting students as they synthesize their responses to the unit's essential question, we recommend using remote support tools that facilitate your ability to respond to them individually, such as one-on-one conferences through Zoom breakout rooms, feedback using Google Docs, or other similar methods of individual interaction. As you select these specific inquiry-based remote learning activities, we encourage you to think about the features and learning goals of each activity and select implementation forms that will help students most effectively engage with that activity. This intentional selection will help maximize students' inquiry-based learning experiences.
Hybrid	To successfully implement inquiry-based learning instruction in a hybrid modality, we recommend focusing on whether students will be learning in person or virtually on specific days and aligning the day's instruction with that modality. Ensuring this alignment will help students engage with and learn from inquiries as effectively as possible. For example, if students are present in person on a day when they respond to an inquiry-based text they're reading, we recommend creating in-class opportunities for them to reflect on their ideas and share verbally with peers, such as reflecting in writing on their ideas and then sharing their thoughts in small-group and whole-class discussions. However, if students are engaging virtually on a day when they respond to the texts they read,

Instructional Modality	Key Suggestions to Consider
	we suggest using remote learning tools to provide them with opportunities to respond to the texts they've read and share those insights with classmates. This purposeful selection of learning tools can facilitate student engagement academic success.
Hyflex	To support student inquiry in hyflex instruction, it's important to construct and implement learning activities that engage students who are joining the class online as well as those who are participating in a face-to-face format. The best hyflex inquiry-based instruction, we feel, allows for students to meaningfully engage in inquiry through either one of these formats. To implement inquiry-based English language arts instruction in a hyflex modality, we recommend constructing learning activities in which students participating online and those participating face-to-face can meet the learning objective. For example, if the objective of a lesson or activity is for students to understand key aspects of inquiry, you can share a video mini-lesson with students who are participating virtually at the same time you share it with those who are joining in person. If students are sharing the results of their inquiries, you can construct ways for all students to do so using technological tools that all students can access. For example, if students give presentations on their inquiries, those presentations can be livestreamed so that all members of the class can learn from their peers and provide feedback. (These presentations can also be recorded so that students who are unable to join the class in real time due to technological challenges or other issues can still see them.) Also, if students create documents about their inquiries such as infographics or one-pagers, they can share them and give feedback to peers via Google Docs so that all students can access those responses whether they engage virtually or in person.

7

Assessing Student Learning

In this chapter, we explore best practices and key ideas to consider related to effective formative and summative assessment in the context of remote English language arts instruction. As we discuss further in the chapter, literacy assessment is a complex and nuanced endeavor: if done well, it cannot be easily simplified or based on measures that prioritize efficiency over usefulness and authenticity (International Literacy Association, 2017). In remote teaching and learning, effective assessment takes on a new dimension as we English language arts teachers must determine the formative and assessment processes that best guide teaching and learning while also aligning with the features of remote instruction. This chapter addresses these topics in a variety of ways. First, we describe key components of remote English language arts assessment, noting what can make these assessments useful and effective. After that, we consider why it's so important to assess students in meaningful and authentic ways in remote contexts. Then we look at an example of Jennifer's assessment-related work with her middle school students. Next, we share recommendations for teachers to consider when assessing student learning remotely. Finally, we discuss how the information described in this chapter can be adapted to fit with a range of modalities.

What Are the Key Aspects of Remote English Language Arts Assessment?

Effective assessment is central to many discussions of effective English language arts instruction. The National Council of Teachers of English (2018) and International Literacy Association (2017) recently published policy statements and briefs about the best practices of assessment—both documents addressed the various forms that assessments can take and the need for literacy assessments can be aligned with their particular instructional contexts. The International Literacy Association's (2017) document "Literacy Assessment: What Everyone Needs to Know" discusses the importance of considering the types of reading and writing being assessed, the assessment's purpose, and the specific students being assessed. Similarly, the National Council of Teachers of English's (2018) position statement "Literacy Assessment: Definitions, Principles, and Practices" asserts that "[l]iteracy assessment is varied and includes multiple measures of different domains, including processes, texts, and reflection" (n.p.).

These ideas about literacy assessment being adapted for specific contexts and purposes are especially relevant to our focus in this book on remote English language arts instruction. As we teach in remote contexts, it's important to keep in mind what types of assessment best align with the features and attributes of remote teaching and learning. With this in mind, this section explores best practices of formative and summative assessment that correspond with English language arts instruction in remote contexts. Let's begin by examining what strong remote formative assessment in literacy instruction can look like.

Formative Assessment

Formative assessment practices, low-stakes assessment practices designed to gauge students' understanding and therefore drive future instruction, are important to English language arts instruction in all teaching and learning formats. In its position statement "Expanding Formative Assessment for Equity and Agency," the National Council of Teachers of English (2020) explains that formative assessment is "a practice of or commitment to frequently checking for understanding and adjusting instruction" (n.p.). We feel that regular and useful formative assessment practices are especially important to remote instruction, in which communication with students takes a variety of forms and differs from traditional in-class interaction. For example, in a synchronous lesson on Zoom, an asynchronous learning activity, or a hybrid or hyflex class session, it can be challenging for teachers to have clear understandings of how students are grasping key content. Because of this, we recommend being as intentional and deliberate as possible when utilizing formative assessment in your remote English language arts instruction.

In addition to in-class applications of knowledge in which students demonstrate their understandings through remote learning tools such as discussion board posts, breakout group conversations, or comments on Google

Docs, we suggest asking students to answer exit questions or complete exit activities at the end of a lesson or learning activity. Students can share their responses to these questions or activities in ways that correspond with your particular remote learning format; for instance, they can share insights in the Zoom chat box, share them on a Google Form or Document, express them on an online discussion board (such as those in platforms like Google Classroom and Canvas), or through the use of another method that best aligns with the features of the context associated with your instruction. By asking students to complete these responses, you will gain regular formative assessment information that you can use to evaluate your students' understandings and guide your future instruction.

Summative Assessment

We feel that the most effective remote English language arts assessment provides students with ways to authentically express and apply the ideas and insights they've gained through their learning experiences. To do this, we teachers can design summative assessments that prioritize the application of knowledge over the recall of information. While the authentic application is a key principle of literacy assessment in general (Dolghan, Kelly, & Zelkha, 2010), we believe it is especially important to effective assessment in remote teaching and learning because of the alignment that exists between the features of remote assessment and the opportunities for students to authentically express and apply their knowledge. For example, since students in remote English language arts instruction are not spending as much (or any) time in the classroom, we can design assessment opportunities in which they are asked to apply the knowledge they've gained and concepts they've considered in ways. In contrast, tests and quizzes in which students recall information are not as aligned with the features of remote instruction because they do not create the opportunities for the authentic application that students can do in their remote learning time.

Authentic English language arts assessments can take a wide range of forms: we recommend providing students with a range of opportunities to demonstrate and apply their knowledge in ways that have applicability to real-world contexts and situations. For example, students could create websites or podcasts on social issues reflected in texts they've read, using the texts as well as other ideas to inform their responses. Similarly, students can write for real-world audiences on topics that matter to them, which will allow the students to not only convey their analyses of those topics but also apply the writing strategies and grammatical concepts they've studied. Students can even work together to create virtual conferences or webinars in which they identify authentic examples or applications of concepts they've studied—these virtual conferences can be conducted among the students or could be shared with wider audiences, such as caregivers, families, and community members. All these authentic applications are ways that facilitate students' abilities to remotely apply and utilize the information they learn in English language arts.

Why Is It Important?

Implementing regular, authentic, and useful assessment is important to strong remote English language arts instruction for a variety of reasons. For instance, the use of consistent formative assessment is especially important to remote teaching because of the way it provides teachers with frequent opportunities to evaluate student progress. We feel these regular, low-stakes assessments are of particular significance in remote contexts in which teachers and students don't have the same opportunities for one-on-one in-person interaction that traditional face-to-face learning provides. In the face-to-face classroom, for example, it can be easier to check in with students to gauge their understanding or to evaluate in an informal way how well students are grasping key content. By asking students to complete remote exit questions or exit activities, we teachers will gather useful and consistent assessment data that we can use to inform our instruction as we guide students' learning.

In addition to the benefits provided by regular remote formative assessments, it's also important to consider the positive features of authentic remote summative assessments, such as those described in the previous section. These opportunities for students to express their understandings of important concepts in ways that align with real-world contexts and situations can increase student motivation by providing opportunities for them to meaningfully apply the information they've learned. Since students have reported lower motivation and academic performance in remote learning (Nierenberg, 2020), engaging and meaningful assessments that mirror real-life applications are especially important in this context. Also, since authentic assessments provide teachers with a great deal of information about how well students are able to apply key concepts and ideas they've learned (Wiggins, 1998), incorporating these types of assessments provides useful information on student learning that can drive future instruction. For example, after we teachers look at the ways students perform on authentic assessment projects and apply key concepts and ideas while doing so, we can use that assessment data to decide on concepts we need to revisit in our future instruction. This connection between summative assessments and future instruction is especially important to remote instruction because it can enhance students' abilities to be academically successful in a potentially challenging learning environment.

Now, let's take a look at Jennifer's work with assessment in her remote English language arts instruction.

Instructional Snapshot: An Example From Jennifer's Work

As a project-based, summative assessment, my students were given a project in which they had to answer the following prompt, provided by my district's curriculum guide:

> Identify a problem in the community or school that needs a hero to bring about positive change. Imagine you are a student activist who is trying to promote positive changes within your school or community. Create a proposal activity for your school or community that would help solve the problem and bring about a solution.

To gain inspiration, we read two articles on youth who helped solve problems within their own communities. The problems we read about our youth targeting were minimizing illiteracy and cleaner parks. The model articles were the perfect way to jump-start my students' thinking.

The project was expected to be completed within the five class days we have class, whether that be virtually or in person. A planning guide was assigned for students to jump-start their thinking. This guide consisted of five questions students had to answer before beginning to write:

1. What is one problem your community or school is facing?
2. What can you do to solve the problem? What is the solution?
3. Has this issue occurred in other communities or schools?
4. Was it solved? If yes, how? If not, why?
5. What programs can I implement (put in place) that can help solve the problem in my community or school?

A writing workshop on thesis statements and unity was presented after students completed their planning guide. An important focus for this project was to have an organized, unified plan of action to solve the problem within the community or school. This begins with a clear thesis statement. We used Pear Deck to review the thesis statement formula and then began sharing our thesis statements. Because Pear Deck is anonymous, we are able to share with our classmates with the fear of judgment, and it allows me to offer verbal suggestions on what to edit. Our workshop continued as we reviewed transitional words and phrases and ways to organize our writing appropriately throughout our different modalities. Students then revised their thesis on their planning guide and moved onto the next stage.

After completing their planning, students were then ready to decide what modality they would complete their project in. The options consisted of a five-paragraph essay, a slideshow, a blog post, a newspaper article, or a brochure. Students were given the freedom to organize their project as they wished, but they had to have a clear thesis statement that identified their school or community's problem, list a clear plan of action, and name any challenges the student may face while trying to solve the problem. The project would be assessed using our state's writing rubric that scores writing based on composition, written expression, and usage and mechanics.

Throughout the process, students met with me to get feedback and guidance on their work. It was shocking how quickly students worked when given the ability to suggest a positive change to their community/school. While they practiced their writing skills, students got to work through what it would take to truly solve the problem. This analysis of their community/school encourages students to examine their surroundings and identify problems they can help find solutions for, even at their age.

Key Recommendations

In this section, we share suggestions to consider when implementing assessment practices in remote English language arts instruction. These recommendations reflect key principles of effective assessment that align with the features and attributes of remote teaching and learning; they are designed to help you put the ideas discussed in this chapter into action in your own remote instruction. They will guide you as you implement context-specific assessment (International Literacy Association, 2017; National Council of Teachers of English, 2018) through thoughtful formative (National Council of Teachers of English, 2020) and authentic summative assessment (Dolghan et al., 2010). Specifically, we recommend following four guidelines when assessing student knowledge in remote learning:

- ◆ Construct formative assessments aligned with the features of remote learning.

- Use remote formative assessments throughout instructional activities and as closure to those activities.
- Provide a range of remote-friendly authentic summative assessment options.
- Ensure alignment between the summative authentic assessment options and key learning objectives.

Now, let's look at each of these recommendations individually by examining what each one can look like in action and why it represents a key component of remote English language arts assessment.

Recommendation One: Construct Formative Assessments Aligned With the Features of Remote Learning

The first recommendation we have for assessing students' remote English language arts learning is to create formative assessments that are aligned with features of remote learning. To construct these assessments, we teachers need to think strategically about two questions: (1) Do these formative assessment tools work well with the remote learning format in which we're teaching? and (2) Do these assessments provide useful information about student learning progress? If we can answer yes to both these questions regarding a particular formative assessment tool, then that tool is an effective one to use. For example, if we're teaching a synchronous class in which all students are participating remotely Zoom, then an effective formative assessment could be for all students to answer a question at the end of class that corresponds with a lesson's key learning goals and share their responses to that question in the Zoom chat box. This type of response corresponds with these questions because it aligns with that particular method of remote instruction and provides the teacher with information about how well students are understanding key content.

Applying this framework to another modality, if an English language teacher is teaching a class taught in a hybrid format in which students are learning in school some days and remotely on others, we can craft formative assessments that align with a given day's features. For example, students might share verbal responses on days in which they participate in school but would need to express their ideas remotely on days they learn outside of school. If students are conducting this remote learning asynchronously, they can share their ideas on Google Docs or Google Forms that provide the teacher with useful formative assessment data. It's essential that we teachers consider the specific remote learning context and the assessments that best align with that context while providing us with useful information about student learning progress.

Recommendation Two: Use Remote Formative Assessments Throughout Instructional Activities and as Closure to Those Activities

As you put into action the ideas described in Recommendation One about the strategic use of remote formative assessment, we recommend doing so at multiple points in the instructional process. Students can demonstrate their knowledge with formative assessments that can be implemented in the middle of an instructional sequence as well through assessments that are used as closure activities at the end of a class period or learning activity. For example, formative assessments that can be implemented during an instructional process could involve written responses that students share remotely to readings they've done or low-stakes writings that they can share with you through a digital platform. Both of these assessments will provide you with useful information aligned with remote instruction about how well students are understanding key concepts related to their English language arts work. We recommend evaluating these formative assessments during the instructional period to the extent possible and then in more depth after class. For instance, if students are completing low-stakes writings in which they apply a certain writing strategy or concept, we suggest giving each piece an overview evaluation during the class time as they submit the pieces and then looking at them in more depth afterward to evaluate student progress and make decisions about what to teach next.

In addition to these in-process formative assessments that students complete in the middle of an instructional sequence, we recommend using low-stakes exit questions and exit activities that students can use to convey their understanding of key concepts and ideas. For example, if students are learning about a particular writing strategy in the day's class, they might answer a question about why authors use that strategy to enhance their works and share their ideas remotely through a format that aligns with the features of your remote teaching and learning. Similarly, if students have focused on analyzing a particular text that day, they can respond to a question that asks them to demonstrate their understanding by commenting on something in that text that especially struck them, connecting the text to another one they've read, or relating the piece to an essential question or big-picture topic. Students can then share these ideas through digital tools such as a Zoom chat box, a Google Doc, a Google Form, an online discussion board, or another resource that aligns with the features of your particular learning context, which will give you quick access to their insights and provide you with useful formative assessment data that can guide your future remote instruction.

Recommendation Three: Provide a Range of Remote-Friendly Authentic Summative Assessment Options

When implementing summative assessments in remote English language arts instruction, we recommend providing students with a range of options to authentically demonstrate their knowledge. As discussed earlier in this chapter, these authentic assessment options can take a range of forms; one especially important aspect of this assessment type is that it gives students opportunities to demonstrate their knowledge through application rather than recall. To make them aligned with remote learning, it's important to reflect on how well specific assessments correspond with the technological tools to which your students have access and will provide them with opportunities to apply their knowledge in meaningful ways. By giving students a range of possible authentic summative assessments from which to choose, we can increase their opportunities for agency and motivation in their academic work.

Figure 7.1 lists and describes some possible authentic summative assessments that we feel can work well in remote teaching and learning. The ideas described in this table are meant to provide useful information on types of assessments that are aligned with remote instruction and the reasons they align with remote instruction.

Recommendation Four: Ensure Alignment Between the Summative Authentic Assessment Options and Key Learning Objectives

When we provide students with a range of authentic summative assessment options like those described in the previous recommendation, it's important that we make sure that all the possible assessments are aligned with key learning objectives that we want to ensure students understand. To do this, it's important that we teachers decide on the central concepts that we want students to show their understandings of and select assessments that will allow them to demonstrate those understandings. Application-based

Assessment	Brief Description	Why It Aligns With Remote Teaching and Learning
Website on a social issue	Students can create websites on social issues reflected in texts they've read, using those texts as support.	This assessment format provides students with authentic opportunities for students to share their ideas in ways that are meant to be created remotely for remote audiences, creating a strong alignment with remote instruction.
Podcast on a social issue	Similar to the previously described websites, students can create podcasts on social issues in the texts they've read and use those texts to support their ideas.	Podcasts can make outstanding remote assessments because they are meant to be shared remotely and align with both individual and collaborative work. For example, students can create podcasts on their own, or they can interview others and remotely incorporate their perspectives.
Writing for real-world audiences	Students can write on issues that matter to them and share those perspectives in authentic ways, such as posting them on Google Docs and sharing those links on social media, writing letters to online newspapers and magazines, and writing blog posts and comments that are read by authentic audiences.	By writing for real-world audiences, students can see that writing is not something just done for school: it can be done to share ideas in authentic, real-world ways. Through doing this, students are able to gain practice and experience with writing concepts while also sharing their perspectives with others who go beyond their teacher and classmates.

Figure 7.1 Possible Authentic Summative Assessments

Assessment	Brief Description	Why It Aligns With Remote Teaching and Learning
Virtual panel conferences and webinars	In virtual panel conferences and webinars, students share ideas about key concepts they've studied and their unique perspectives on these ideas. Students present on concepts that are thematically aligned but offer their unique perspectives on these issues.	These panels and webinars provide excellent opportunities for remote learning evaluation because they create ways for students to express ideas and apply key understandings. This assessment format aligns well with culturally relevant and inquiry-based instruction because it provides excellent opportunities for students to provide their unique perspectives on conceptually aligned topics.
Infographics and one-pagers	Infographics and one-pagers are documents that use graphics and images to express key ideas about a character, text, theme, or concept. They allow students to combine words and images to effectively convey their ideas.	These documents, through their combination of visual features and student-created texts, purposefully incorporate digital tools in ways that call for students to express their knowledge. They are created and shared online in ways that align with features of remote learning and provide teachers with clear understandings of how well students have grasped key content.

Figure 7.1 (Continued)

authentic assessments align well with this goal, as they provide students with a range of ways to demonstrate key understandings. For example, students could use many of the assessments described in Recommendation Three to demonstrate mastery of essential learning objectives. A key component of this process is to decide on important learning goals that students can show their understanding of in a variety of ways. For instance, students can convey their mastery of an important idea, topic, or concept through a website, a podcast, an infographic, a one-pager, or another format.

When giving students a range of ways to demonstrate their understanding, it's important to convey to them the key objectives that they'll need to show mastery of regardless of the format they select. For instance, if students are examining a societal issue and its relation to texts they've read, we educators can emphasize to them that they'll show their knowledge of this issue and the texts they studied through any assessment option they select. It's a good idea to provide students with a list of key topics or concepts they'll need to show their understanding of regardless of the summative assessment option they pick. This can ensure consistent assessment and provide you with important information about student learning that can guide your future instruction.

Adapting for a Range of Modalities

When implementing the remote English language arts assessment ideas and strategies discussed in this chapter, it's important to reflect on the range of possible modalities and make assessment-related decisions aligned with the ways you and your students are working. Because of the importance of alignment between assessment forms and learning modalities, this section provides insights to consider when implementing this chapter's assessment-related insights in a range of instructional modalities: entirely remote instruction (in which instruction is completely virtual), hybrid instruction (in which students are physically present in the classroom some days and engage through virtual learning other days), and hyflex instruction (in which some students are physically present in the classroom and other students join at the same time virtually). By sharing these insights, we aim to provide you with suggestions and information that can help you utilize instructional practices that fit well with the instructional modality used in your instruction.

Instructional Modality	Key Suggestions to Consider
Entirely remote	When assessing students who are learning entirely remotely, it's important that we reflect carefully on the remote learning tools that our students have available to them and how each one of those tools can align with the kind of assessment information we want to gather and analyze. For example, if our assessment goal is to collect formative assessment information at the end of a class period or

Instructional Modality	Key Suggestions to Consider
	instructional sequence that shows how well students have grasped a key concept, we'll want to select an assessment form that aligns with that objective and with the features of remote learning available to our students. Similarly, if we have the summative assessment goal of determining students' mastery of writing strategies we've taught them, it would be in our best interest to select an assessment method that provides students with opportunities to demonstrate this expertise remotely. While aspects of these remote assessments will certainly vary based on what our students have learned and what remote resources they have available, the most important aspect of assessing using this modality is the alignment between the assessment forms used, the concepts being assessed, and the available resources.
Hybrid	Since students who participate in hybrid instruction engage in are physically present in the classroom some days and participate in remote learning on others, we recommend aligning assessments with the features of the ways students are engaging on a particular day. When conducting formative assessments, in which you'll use students' insights from a class session or learning activity to gauge their understanding, we suggest making assessment decisions based on how students are learning that day. When students are learning remotely, we recommend selecting ways for them to demonstrate their insights using features of remote learning that are available to them. Similarly, when students are participating in person, they can convey their understandings through exit question responses and class discussions they can share in class. When asking students to complete summative assessments, we suggest aligning the features of the assessment with the ways students will participate on the day the assessment will be submitted. If students will be participating

Instructional Modality	Key Suggestions to Consider
	remotely on the day an assessment is due, we recommend giving them assessment options that align with remote learning activities and resources. In contrast, if students will be attending class in person on the day they share summative assessments, we can provide them with assessment options that correspond with that form of engagement. It is also possible to give students options of completing assessments that can be submitted remotely or in person. We teachers can then allow students to submit those assessments remotely or in person based on what best aligns with the assessment they select.
Hyflex	Since hyflex instruction involves all students participating in class at the same time—some in person and others remotely—we recommend selecting formative and summative assessment tools with which students can engage regardless of where they are. For example, students can share formative assessment results and insights through Zoom chat features, Google Docs, or online discussion boards whether they are physically present in the classroom or engaging remotely. This will give you as the teacher consistent and useful formative assessment information that you can evaluate regardless of how students are participating. Similarly, students can share their summative assessments using technological tools that all students can access whether they are engaging in person or remotely. For example, if a student chooses to create a website on a social issue and uses texts examined in class to inform their understanding of this issue, that student could share the website with their peers whether they are engaging in person or remotely. In addition, a student who writes a piece for an authentic audience could share this work with classmates through Zoom or a similar platform in ways that can be accessed remotely and in person.

Teacher Roles in a New World

A Note About This Chapter and the Others in This Section
This chapter and the two that follow it compose Section III, "Teacher Roles in a New World." The ideas in this section are designed to guide and support teachers as they navigate the unique challenges of the remote learning environment. While the previous chapters in this book address specific instructional tactics and ideas, Chapters 8, 9, and 10 focus on big-picture ideas and recommendations that are essential to remote instruction, such as communicating, reflecting, and taking care of yourself. As we explore in these chapters, these concepts are important to teaching in general but are especially significant to remote English language arts instruction given the specific challenges and attributes of that instruction.

8

Strategies for Communication With Students and Caregivers

In this chapter, we examine key strategies that can facilitate effective remote communication with our English language arts students and their caregivers. While strong communication with students and caregivers is important to effective teaching and learning in general, we feel that it takes on extra significance in remote instruction. Because remote learning has reduced or eliminated the amount of face-to-face contact and corresponding interaction that was present during in-person school, effective and meaningful communication about what students are learning and the best ways for them to succeed has become increasingly difficult. Due to this challenge, we feel it is important to be as intentional as possible about the ways we communicate with our students and their caregivers about curriculum, assignments, students' academic progress, and opportunities for support.

This chapter provides four recommendations that English language arts teachers can utilize during remote learning to facilitate the effectiveness of communication with students and their caregivers about academic content and student learning:

- Create an online class page that houses important information designed to help students succeed.
- Share weekly agendas that describe what students will learn.
- Provide caregivers with regular newsletters that communicate important information.
- Hold remote conversations with caregivers that illustrate what students learn.

When describing these recommendations, we discuss what each one is and why it is especially important in the context of remote instruction. Now, let's get started on our exploration of ways to maximize the communication with your students and their caregivers during remote learning.

Recommendation One: Create an Online Class Page That Houses Important Information Designed to Help Students Succeed

Our first recommendation for facilitating effective communication with students and their caregivers is to create an online class page or website that is used to house important information that will help facilitate student success. The specific components of this online page can take a variety of forms. For example, based on your school's learning management system, you may have a page in a system such as Google Classroom or Canvas that is specifically dedicated to the material you teach and your students learn. If your school does not have a subscription to such a system, you can make a free website through platforms such Weebly, Wix, and others. No matter what platform or system you use to construct your website, the most important aspect of the site is that it contains resources and information that will guide students as they complete remote academic work for your English language arts course. For example, the site can contain assignment descriptions and rubrics to which students can refer as they work on summative assessments. In addition, you can use the site to store videos you create that explain key concepts, such as a video mini-lesson on important literacy strategies to which students can refer repeatedly. A class website can be an excellent way to house materials that students need, making life easier for them and saving you time: if students need access to important course information, they'll know to look for it on the website (Ruday, 2018).

While class websites are outstanding tools for organized and student-friendly English language arts courses in general, they are especially useful for remote teaching and learning. Without the benefit of a structured classroom space that students regularly use, it can be extra difficult to structure the information and resources to which students have access. For example, students working in a face-to-face setting will have regular physical access to materials, tools, and resources that a teacher has set up. Since remote learning often involves students setting up their own learning environments, it's especially important that we teachers create well-structured and clearly organized resources students and their caregivers can use to find important course information. Without this access, students and caregivers can become frustrated and anxious, especially given the existing challenges already associated with remote learning. However, with a well-organized and informative website that contains important and easy-to-find course materials, we can help our students succeed and facilitate their caregivers' abilities to support them.

Recommendation Two: Share Weekly Agendas That Describe What Students Will Learn

Along with constructing a website that houses important resources to guide student learning and organization, we recommend sharing with students and their caregivers weekly agendas that discuss what content students will learn that week and what resources they'll need. These agendas, which "are outlines of the material covered for the week and the homework and assignments relevant to each day" (Ruday, 2018, p. 199), provide students with clear information about academic expectations, the work to be done, and the resources they'll need to complete that work. In addition to informing students about important academic work, agendas facilitate caregivers' abilities to support their students: because they provide important information about what students will be doing academically in a particular week and what they'll need to do to complete that work, caregivers can use these agendas to help their students stay on track and check in with them to ensure that the work is completed. With the information these weekly agendas provide, students will have the information they need to complete academic work, and caregivers will have the details necessary to support them.

These weekly agendas are especially useful in the context of remote learning, where students do not have the same routines and supports that in-person school provides. By providing students with clear expectations and caregivers with key details about exactly what learning activities are taking place that week, we teachers can provide important details that can facilitate academic success and clear communication during remote learning. We recommend emailing the agendas to students and caregivers at the beginning of each week and posting them on the course website to ensure that everyone involved will have easy access. Making this information readily available remotely will help students be able to access it if they have questions, miss an instructional day, or need to remind themselves of important upcoming work. Caregivers can also access the information when they want to check on what work is assigned for the course and how their students are progressing with that work.

Recommendation Three: Provide Caregivers With Regular Newsletters That Communicate Important Information

In addition to sending students weekly agendas that identify key material to be covered, we recommend creating a course newsletter that you regularly provide to caregivers. These newsletters, which discuss important topics recently discussed in the course as well as upcoming assignments and events (Ruday, 2018), are great tools for facilitating strong communication with caregivers. While the weekly agendas described in the previous recommendation provide important information, these newsletters provide additional detail and context that can further develop the sense of communication and support between you as the teacher and students' caregivers. When constructing these newsletters in the past, Sean has divided them into the categories of "What We've Been Up To" and "What's Coming Up," with separate relevant sections related to particular components of literacy instruction, such as reading, writing, and word study (Ruday, 2018). The newsletters can foster a strong sense of communication and let students' caregivers know that you are committed to keeping them informed of key developments in their students' learning. We recommend sending these newsletters to students' caregivers weekly or biweekly via email to further create a sense of regular communication and support.

We feel that these newsletters are especially important to the context of remote instruction because of the way they facilitate clear and detailed communication between us as teachers and students' caregivers. During remote teaching and learning, it can be more difficult for caregivers to feel connected to their students' teachers and to understand what has been and will be taking place in their students' learning experiences. By sending regular newsletters to our students' caregivers, we teachers clearly convey that we want to build strong relationships with those caregivers during a time when authentic connections can be difficult to create. Regular newsletters are excellent ways to create strong communication with caregivers during any form of instruction but are especially useful for establishing meaningful connections and sharing important information during the challenging time of remote learning.

Recommendation Four: Hold Remote Conversations With Caregivers That Illustrate What Students Learn

This recommendation represents a way for us teachers to show caregivers what their students are or will be learning in their remote English language arts instruction. Katie Van Sluys (2011) describes an example of this in which a school adopted a workshop and process-based approach to writing instruction; since many students' caregivers were unfamiliar with this approach, the school provided them with opportunities to see what this instructional practice looked like in action and shared with them its key components. This approach can be applied to all aspects of English language arts instruction: when you are implementing a new instructional practice with which caregivers may be unfamiliar, it's a great idea to invite them to a discussion on that topic. In this discussion, we recommend talking with students' caregivers about the essential features and benefits of the instructional approach you'll implement in your teaching. Doing so can help caregivers understand the instructional methods you'll use and how to support their students if they need extra help. In the context of remote instruction, these conversations can take place virtually to ensure social distance and safety.

We feel that these instructional conversations with caregivers are especially significant during remote learning. Through these conversations, we educators can talk with caregivers about what their English language arts instruction will look like in remote contexts. Since remote teaching and learning is new for many so stakeholders in education (such as teachers, students, and caregivers), we can increase caregivers' understanding of what their students will be doing and learning in school through remote conversations about what students will learn and how they'll learn it. For example, if students will be engaging in inquiry-based instruction and analysis, we can hold a remote conversation with caregivers that describes what this instructional practice is, how it will look in remote teaching and learning, what students will do as part of it, and how caregivers can support their students.

Final Thoughts on Communicating With Students and Caregivers

As the recommendations and ideas discussed in this chapter illustrate, there are a number of important and useful ways for us to communicate with our students and their caregivers during remote learning. These practices are effective ways to facilitate strong communication in any educational context but are especially important in the context of remote teaching and learning, in which communication can be both extra challenging and significant. Communication can be particularly challenging in remote learning because the features of many remote learning formats eliminate the regular routine and structure associated with face-to-face contact and in-person classrooms. Because of these challenges and changes, it is especially important that we are strategic and purposeful when communicating with our students and their caregivers during remote English language arts instruction. The information in this chapter will help you communicate with those important individuals in strategic, purposeful, and beneficial ways.

9

Reflecting on Technology

As we've engaged in remote instruction, we have continually reflected on ideas and issues related to the role of technology in our teaching and our students' learning. While technology has played an important role in English language arts instruction for years (Richards, 2000; Swenson, Rozema, Young, McGrail, & Whitin, 2005), we feel it has taken on even more significance in the time of increased remote teaching and learning. Since remote instruction has taken on a greater role in education, we believe it is essential for us teachers to reflect on its role in our pedagogical practices. When we reflect on the topic of technology and its role in remote English language arts instruction, we find ourselves thinking about the importance of technology use being both strategic and equitable. In this chapter, we explore both these ideas, focusing on the importance of technology use in remote English language arts instruction that is purposefully selected to align key instructional goals and equitable for students' technological access, experience levels, and individual needs.

Reflection 1: Strategic Technology Use

As educators, we've definitely felt overwhelmed by the many technological tools and resources that we hear and read about. During remote learning, this experience has increased: it seems to us like there is almost always a new instructional technology feature that is being discussed or advertised in teacher-focused environments. While many technological tools and ideas can be beneficial for effective teaching and learning, we recommend starting your technology-based decision-making process by reflecting on your instructional goals and students, not specific innovations. As we discuss in this book's introduction, instead of deciding on a particular technological resource and designing instruction that fits that program, we suggest first identifying what you want to teach your students and then selecting the technological tools that you feel will best help your students reach the learning objectives you've established.

By selecting technological tools strategically, you'll work to ensure that you're making the choices that best align with the material you're teaching your students and the students themselves, matching the technology in your teaching with "students, instruction, and curricular goals" (Young & Bush, 2004, p. 9). If we educators feel that a particular technology resource will have positive impacts on these three essential components of our pedagogy, we can be confident that we've made strong decisions related to the uses of technology in our teaching. Conversely, if we're not sure if a technology tool is a good way to reach our students, facilitate our instruction, and achieve our curricular goals, then it's in our best interest to further reflect on that resource and determine if it's the resource we should use. If not, we can consider other possible tools and decide on one that will best align with all our pedagogical elements. Without careful reflection on the benefits and uses of available technological resources, we can find ourselves in situations in which technology is used for the sake of doing instead of because it is the best tool to achieve a particular learning outcome (Pasternak, 2007).

While the strategic selection of technological tools is important to effective English language arts instruction in general, we feel that this approach is especially important to remote teaching and learning. Because of the digital nature of remote instruction, teachers are being asked to consider a wide range of technological resources and tools, many of which may be new to them. When we educators examine many new forms of technology, it's especially important that we keep in mind the features of those tools and how they optimize the effectiveness of our teaching. As part of this consideration and reflection, it's important that we think about the many features of specific technological resources and how those features do or do not align with specific aspects of our instruction. For example, when incorporating Zoom into instruction, we can maximize its usefulness to our teaching and our students' learning if we look at its many aspects and make strategic decisions about those aspects. Zoom's chat feature, for instance, is a useful tool in specific aspects of remote instruction, such as when we're holding a synchronous remote or hybrid class and want students to share brief responses. On the other hand, if we're looking for a technological tool that aligns with longer student responses that take more time to compose, we might use Google Docs or online discussion boards. Through the strategic and reflective selection of technological resources, we can maximize our remote English language arts instruction in ways that help our students succeed.

Reflection 2: Equitable Technology Implementation

Like the concept of strategic technology use described in the preceding section, equitable technology access is an essential issue for us educators to carefully consider during remote instruction. In order for us to create effective remote English language arts contexts designed to help facilitate student success, we need to reflect on ways to make our instructional technology equitable regarding a number of important issues, such as students' technological access, experience levels, and individual needs. In this section, we look at each of these concepts and explore why they are important to equitable technology implementation in remote English language arts instruction.

Students' Technological Access

An essential concept to consider when reflecting on the issue of equity in remote learning is that students have a range of levels of technological access. In a 2020 *Education Week* article titled "Closing COVID-19 Equity Gaps in Schools," author Christine A. Samuels calls for schools to "[c]lose the digital divide to ensure that all students have access to devices, internet, and technology support" in a section titled "Prioritizing Educational Equity." As teachers, it is important that we are aware that our students may have different levels of access related to these topics. We can use this awareness to inform our communication with students and their caregivers as well as our instruction. For example, we can remind students and caregivers of any technological and accessibility supports that the school provides students and families, such as those that Samuels describes. In addition, we can build variation and flexibility into our instruction that account for different levels of students' technological access. One such way is by providing students who may not be able to join synchronous classes due to technological access issues with alternate ways to learn information and convey their knowledge. For example, students could complete asynchronous assignments that may involve reading articles, reflecting on them, and watching short prerecorded videos if their technology allows. These students could then share their ideas and responses via technological tools that require less bandwidth, such as emails, online discussion boards, or Google Docs. Of course, this is just one potential example: the specific tactics you'll use to support your students will depend on their individual situations and the assignments you give them. While certain aspects of these features will vary across contexts, we strongly encourage you to keep in mind that students may have different levels of access to technology and to factor this issue into your instructional decision-making.

Students' Technological Experience Levels

In addition to reflecting on students' technological access and making appropriate accommodations in our instruction and communication with students, it is also important that we recognize that our students may have different levels of experience with technological tools and programs. This variation in experience is another form of the "digital divide" that Christine Samuels (2020) refers to in the previously mentioned article "Closing COVID-19 Equity Gaps in Schools." Our awareness of the potential variation in students' experience will help us facilitate equitable instruction based on understandings of this concept. We can incorporate this awareness into our instruction in multiple ways. At the beginning of the school year, we can ask students to complete surveys seen only by us in which they assess their comfort with various technological tools and innovations. We can then use these survey results to support our students and even decide which tools we want to use in our instruction. When we implement technological tools and resources in our teaching, it's important that we take some time to familiarize students with those innovations and how to use them and to answer questions they have. By doing this, we can ensure students' common understandings about technological tools and avoid assumptions about students' experience and familiarity levels. While students work, we can then check in with them individually about their comfort with technological tools and provide them with the support that will help them use those resources.

Students' Individual Needs

In order to reflect on equitable and student-centered technology use in remote English language arts instruction, we also need to consider students' individual needs and how we can use technological tools and resources to meet those needs. Since the specific learning needs of your students will be unique to them, we encourage you to communicate with those students, their caregivers, school administrators, and others involved to identify the best ways to meet their needs during remote instruction. The website Educating All Learners (2020)—www.educatingalllearners.org—provides a number of resources related to making remote teaching and learning as accessible as possible to all students, including those with disabilities, explaining that "[a]s schools shift to online learning, the needs of students with disabilities are too often put on the back burner—instead, they must be considered from the beginning" (para. 2). Some practices that we recommend incorporating to help all students learn are using captioning on videos to help all students access the material, holding one-on-one conferences with students as they work on remote assessments to provide them with individualized support, and being flexible with the amount of processing and work time students are able to take on projects. These are some overarching suggestions that can help remote instruction align with students' needs. The additional and more specific steps you'll take in your instruction will be based on your students and the best ways to support them as individual learners.

Final Thoughts

The technology-related issues discussed in this chapter have long been part of the conversation about effective teaching but have taken on special significance during the time of increased remote instruction. We encourage you to think carefully and reflectively about the technological choices you make during your remote English language arts instruction. This thoughtful reflection will help you build an equitable learning experience for your students. When we align our technology use with key learning goals and think carefully about issues of equity in our technology implementation, we work to create meaningful and inclusive remote instruction. There are so many forms of remote technology use and implementation options available to us teachers in today's educational context. The reflective ideas described in this chapter will help you incorporate them in ways that facilitate student learning, access, and equity.

10

Taking Care of Yourself

The stress (Gallup, 2014) and potential burnout (Richards, 2012) of teachers have long been issues in education. Now, in the current context of remote teaching and learning in the COVID-19 era, this issue has become even more significant: teachers are experiencing "immense challenges, and exhaustion" (Singer, 2020, para. 6). brought on by the intense demands of teaching remotely in a pandemic-altered world. Since the already-significant challenge of taking care of oneself as a teacher has grown in difficulty with increased remote instruction and the associated stressors of COVID-19, we believe that it's especially important that teachers are intentional about focusing on self-care during this time. In this chapter, we share five recommendations regarding ways to create work–life balance, take care of yourself, and manage the stresses associated with remote teaching:

1. Don't wait to engage in self-care activities.
2. Schedule times to disconnect.
3. Create time to share and vent about your experiences.
4. Create times to socialize about anything but teaching.
5. Get lost in a passion.

By implementing these recommendations in ways that align with your interests and preferred self-care activities, you take important steps to ensure that you take care of yourself, which will ultimately maximize your productivity, enjoyment, and longevity as a teacher (Ruday, 2018). Now, let's reflect on these suggestions, why they're useful, and how they can enhance your work as a remote English language arts teacher.

Recommendation One: Don't Wait to Engage in Self-Care Activities

Sometimes, we teachers might think of self-care activities as things to help us decompress and re-center when we get stressed and overwhelmed. While this can certainly be true, we also encourage you to think of self-care activities as things to do on a regular basis before you experience those feelings. This approach makes our participation in self-care activities proactive instead of reactive and can increase the likelihood that we'll participate in those activities. For example, if someone's go-to self-care tactic is yoga, it would not be in their best interest to wait until they get stressed to do yoga. By doing it regularly, before feeling anxious or overwhelmed, they can ensure that they engage in their self-care activities, which can then ultimately help them deal better with stressors they might encounter. These practices establish a proactive routine that will help us continuously engage in self-care and regularly achieve all these benefits that self-care practices provide. Of course, it's also a good idea to take additional self-care measures when feeling stressed. The recommendation we focus on here is to make sure to participate in some self-care activities before stress sets in to proactively take care of yourself and help you get in a regular routine of doing so.

Recommendation Two: Schedule Times to Disconnect

Another proactive self-care tactic we recommend is scheduling times to disconnect from all teaching-related communication, such as email, notifications from learning management systems, and other similar messages. While scheduling times to disconnect from work is important in general, we feel that this is especially important in the context of remote instruction. Because of the digital nature of remote instruction, it's so easy to feel like we educators are always at work. We may receive emails and notifications at all hours of the day, and it's possible to feel called to respond to those messages as soon as we get them. Because of this, we feel that it's essential to delineate times in which you are disconnected from all work-related communication. You might want to use this time to enjoy a self-care activity or just use it for anything at all. For example, Sean will disconnect and work out, read a book, play the Xbox with his 13-year-old, or participate in another activity altogether. No matter what you choose to do during this time, the most important aspect of this recommendation is to be as proactive and regular as possible about scheduling times to disconnect from teaching-related communication to take care of yourself and give yourself a break from the continued pressures and expectations of remote learning.

Recommendation Three: Create Time to Share and Vent About Your Experiences

While it's important to unplug and take time away from the pressures and stresses of remote English language arts instruction, we also recommend creating time to share and vent about your experiences, challenges, frustrations, and successes. Depending on your preferences, you might want to do this with fellow teachers or with others who are not involved in teaching. Whether or not the individuals with whom you share are educators, it's important to find a group of people with whom you feel safe, comfortable, and able to share key aspects of the remote instruction experience. Since so many components of remote teaching are new and challenging, we recommend taking the time to discuss and process your experiences with others. Doing so will create opportunities to express the challenges you're experiencing and can create a sense of community that can help all involved feel supported in a challenging time. You may even want to develop multiple communities by reaching out to teachers at other schools, former colleague classmates, friends, and relatives. In today's world, we can use features like Zoom, FaceTime, and the like to communicate with others and benefit from the opportunities for interaction they provide.

Recommendation Four: Create Times to Socialize About Anything But Teaching

This recommendation works with the ideas in Recommendation Three to emphasize the importance of purposeful communication to self-care. While we believe, as discussed in Recommendation Three, that it's important to take time to vent and talk about the challenges associated with remote teaching, we also feel that it's important that educators create times to socialize about anything but teaching. Although we're extremely passionate about teaching and love discussing issues and topics related to education, we believe that socializing about other topics goes a long way toward avoiding burnout. Since so many teachers are experiencing symptoms of burnout during remote learning in the time of COVID-19 (Singer, 2020), we recommend engaging in social activities that will create opportunities for you to talk about other interests and take your mind off of education-related stresses. These conversations about non-work-related topics can provide balance and rest in a stressful time when both of those entities can be difficult to find.

Recommendation Five: Get Lost in a Passion

To take care of ourselves amidst the challenges and pressures of remote instruction, we recommend immersing yourself in something that you're passionate about and enjoy. By engaging in something you love doing, you can bring yourself joy and excitement, which can help you feel rejuvenated and able to take on challenging tasks. While these specific passions will take on different forms for many of us, the key component they'll all have in common is the way they allow the individual who is interested in that topic to focus on and derive enjoyment from that activity. So, whether you love watching baking shows, listening to a particular musical artist, reading page-turning works by a favorite author, knitting, playing a video game with friends, or anything else, we encourage you to devote some time to engaging in that passion. The feeling of joy and escape that these activities can help you feel happy and rested, which can then help you approach difficult situations as effectively as possible.

Final Thoughts

In order to be effective teachers during remote instruction, it's essential that we take care of ourselves. While it can be easy to forget to prioritize self-care, we strongly recommend making it a point to take care of yourself. The ideas discussed in this chapter about proactively and purposefully engaging in self-care can help us educators guard against feeling overwhelmed, exhausted, and stressed while teaching remotely. When putting these ideas into action in your own life, we encourage you to take time and reflect on the activities that can give you joy and help you feel energized. Once you've identified those activities, we recommend leaning into them as key self-care practices. We strongly believe that self-care makes us as educators more effective for our students: by taking care of ourselves, we'll have the energy, patience, and clarity to be as effective as possible for our students. In other words, it will help us educators be the great teachers that we are capable of being.

IV
Resources

11

Key Takeaway Ideas

Now that you've read the first ten chapters of this book, you've developed a wide range of ideas and practices to use when optimizing the effectiveness of remote English language arts instruction. The insights and approaches we've shared are designed to help you and your students engage in meaningful remote instruction that engages students, centers their positionalities, values equity, helps them learn important content, and aligns with the features of remote teaching and learning. With these core ideas in mind, we present in this chapter five key takeaway ideas to reflect on as you put the insights and examples described in this book into action in your instruction:

- Reflect on and purposefully select technological tools.
- Prioritize community building in remote instruction.
- Emphasize collaboration and interaction.
- Center students' ideas and experiences.
- Be purposeful about communication and self-care.

These recommendations are designed to synthesize important ideas in this book and provide key concluding ideas to keep in mind during your remote English language arts instruction. As you examine them, we recommend thinking about how you'll implement each of these suggestions into your teaching, drawing on the ideas and examples shared in this book. Now, let's jump into these recommendations and consider each of them in detail.

Recommendation One: Reflect On and Purposefully Select Technological Tools

One of the most important aspects of effective remote English language arts instruction is reflecting on and purposefully selecting technological tools. As we've discussed in this book, there are so many apps, programs, and innovations available to teachers engaging in remote teaching and learning that it's easy to feel overwhelmed by the seemingly countless options. These many possibilities not only can result in teachers feeling anxious about which ones to pick but also can make it difficult to select the technological tools that best align with student learning. To address this issue, we strongly recommend reflecting on which resources best align with learning goals and student needs and then selecting tools that correspond with those concepts.

These learning goals and student needs can take a range of forms, such as the instructional objectives you want your students to understand, the ways you want them to demonstrate their knowledge, and how the instructional activities you want them to use align with the modality in which students are working. For example, if your instructional goal is for students to think about and respond to key issues in a text they've read, we recommend thinking about the remote learning tools that you feel best align with this practice and how those tools work in the modality you and your students are using. Google Docs, for instance, can be effective ways for students who are sharing ideas in a synchronous remote class to reflect on and express detailed insights about a topic because students can see their peers' responses come through in real time and respond immediately. In contrast, if students are doing this activity in a remote asynchronous modality, online discussion boards can work well—this technological resource facilitates thoughtful responses that students can share with one another and respond to over a period. The technological resources you use will certainly vary based on specific contextual elements; we encourage you to carefully and thoughtfully reflect on the tools you use to ensure that they best align with important learning goals and student needs.

Recommendation Two: Prioritize Community Building in Remote Instruction

We strongly recommend making community building a point of emphasis in your remote English language arts instruction. While creating a learning community certainly takes on a different form in remote teaching and learning than it does in a traditional in-person classroom, it is still an essential aspect of students' academic and personal successes for a variety of reasons. The relationships we build with our students can make a significant impact on the quality of their experiences in school and maximize their academic performance (Quin, 2016). When we construct strong and supportive learning environments for our students, we can help them feel safe, collaborate with others, and take risks (Aspen Institute, 2017). These benefits of community building are even more important when we consider that students report that they've experienced less motivation and academic success in remote learning (Nierenberg, 2020). By building a strong community of learners in our remote instruction, we can help our students succeed academically through supportive communities that facilitate their abilities to take risks and feel safe.

To intentionally and purposefully construct a learning community that maximizes students' feelings of support and academic success, we recommend reflecting on the essential aspects that you feel should be present in a strong learning community and then thinking about how those components would look in a remote context. For example, if one component that you greatly value in a learning community is the opportunity for students to get to know each other by sharing their opinions about topics that matter to them, you can ask students fun, get-to-know-you questions in the Zoom chat box, on Google Classroom, or through another technological resource before or after class. If something that you believe makes a strong learning community is the opportunity for students to incorporate their own interests into assignments, you can construct remote learning projects in which students have choice and opportunities to express their interests. In addition, if you value a community in which the teacher expresses their authentic personality with the class, you can build in opportunities during mini-lessons and class discussions to share your interests and help your students get to know you as a person. When we build strong remote learning communities, we are seeking to create a supportive learning environment in which students feel safe; while such a community will look different than an in-person one, the core idea of supporting our students remains consistent.

Recommendation Three: Emphasize Collaboration and Interaction

This recommendation builds off the ideas discussed in Recommendation Two: as you build a strong and supportive learning community with your students, we suggest purposefully emphasizing collaboration and interaction in your remote English language arts instruction. Opportunities for students to engage in meaningful collaboration and learning-related conversations are important to effective learning in general (Hurst et al., 2013) and are especially significant to remote learning (Kyei-Blankson et al., 2019), in which students don't have the same natural opportunities for interaction and discussion with classmates and teachers that exist in traditional face-to-face learning. By providing our students with collaborative and interactive experiences, we can help them experience the benefits of being in a supportive and motivational learning community that contains meaningful opportunities for interaction.

The collaborative and interactive work in which students participate can take a range of forms; we recommend purposefully varying the structures of these activities based on the goals of the activities. For example, some collaborative work that students complete together is well suited to the features of Google Docs or Google Slides, others might be best aligned with a breakout room, while others might work best with responses written in a chat box. We believe that all these collaboration tools can provide beneficial experiences for students and do not feel that any specific tool is better than others: rather, we feel that the best collaboration resource to use is the one that best aligns with a particular assignment, your students, and the instructional modality you and your students use. No matter the specific form your students' collaboration takes, we recommend talking with students about how to use the collaboration and why that tool will help them collaborate in ways that align with the assignment. By sharing this information, you'll ensure that your students have clear expectations for the activity, and you'll build a transparent and purposeful instructional environment that will help students understand the benefits that will come from the activities in which they're engaging.

Recommendation Four: Center Students' Ideas and Experiences

An important component of building a student-centered, motivational, and equitable remote learning environment is centering students' ideas and experiences in our instructional practices. To do this, we recommend focusing on the key principles of culturally relevant (Ladson-Billings, 1995) and culturally sustaining pedagogy (Paris, 2012) described in Chapter 5, as well as the inquiry-based approach discussed in Chapter 6. These pedagogical approaches place students' authentic experiences in central roles in the English language arts curriculum. Culturally relevant and sustaining pedagogy facilitates authentic connections between concepts that students learn in school and their out-of-school lives, creating space for students by recognizing and valuing their realities, perspectives, and identities (Lyiscott, 2019) and incorporating the literacies that are authentic to their lived experiences (Duncan-Andrade & Morrell, 2005). Similarly, inquiry-based English language arts instruction's focus on big-picture, thought-provoking essential questions (McTighe & Wiggins, 2013) creates natural opportunities to craft student-centered learning experiences, especially since these questions can be easily and closely aligned with students' curiosities and interests (Ruday & Caprino, 2021).

Fortunately, the structure of remote teaching and learning can create opportunities for students to learn in their own communities and investigate topics that matter to them individually. In remote instruction, students spend more time learning in their homes and communities than they would in a traditional face-to-face context; we teachers can use this feature to construct additional ways for students to bring their communities, cultures, and interests into their learning. For instance, if students are engaging in an activity in which they look for examples of a writing strategy in their out-of-school lives, we can encourage them to look at the many forms of text that exist around them in organic and authentic ways in their communities. This community-based application can work toward culturally relevant and sustaining pedagogy and create a learning environment for students in which the concept of "text" has authentic applications that go beyond what is present in school. Similarly, when students investigate inquiries that center essential questions related to issues in their lives and communities, they can draw on texts from and related to topics that matter to them. Students can then remotely share these ideas, connections, and responses through tools and features of remote learning.

Recommendation Five: Be Purposeful About Communication and Self-Care

To maximize your productivity, effectiveness, and health during the stresses and challenges of remote teaching and learning, we recommend being purposeful and proactive regarding the important topics of communication and self-care. By taking intentional and thoughtful measures in relation to these concepts, we educators can build strong and supportive relationships with our students and their caregivers while also ensuring that we take care of ourselves. While there are certainly differences between communicating effectively with others and engaging in self-care, we feel that there are also important similarities between these actions: they both require purposeful action and they both contribute to our overall well-being and effectiveness, thereby helping us teach well in a difficult time.

When we communicate effectively with our students and their caregivers, we can create smooth and positive learning experiences for all involved. If we provide them with clear information and organized structures in which that information is conveyed, they'll know where to go to find important course details and will be able to use the structures you've created to answer questions on their own. If students and caregivers can do this efficiently and independently, you'll be able to spend more time on your instruction and less time answering questions. In other words, proactive and purposeful communication can increase our efficiency and effectiveness. Similarly, this approach can be applied to self-care strategies: by taking care of ourselves using the tactics and recommendations described in Chapter 10, we can ensure that we're prioritizing our mental and physical health before we feel overwhelmed and stressed. We encourage you to create communication and self-care plans so that you can proactively address the challenges and maximize your effectiveness and health.

Final Thoughts

We wrote this book with two primary goals in mind: (1) to help teachers think about the best ways to teach English language arts and (2) to provide recommendations, ideas, and examples to help teachers put these ideas into action in their remote instruction. The information you've examined in this book will help you achieve these two goals; the range of topics we describe in this text and the variety of recommendations we share are designed to provide a comprehensive perspective on how to maximize the effectiveness of your remote English language arts instruction. By putting these ideas into action, you'll make purposeful instructional choices that center your students and are informed by strategic selections of remote learning tools that align with key learning goals, your individual students, and the instructional modalities that you and your students are working with. We know that remote teaching is not easy, but the information we share in this book about effective English language arts instruction, what it can look like in remote contexts, and how to implement it in your own practice will guide you as you support your students. Now that you've completed this book, we hope that you're able to say, "I know about high-quality English language arts instruction and I know how to implement it in remote learning!"

References

Aspen Institute. (2017). *Putting it all together*. The Aspen Institute's National Commission on Social, Emotional, and Academic Development. Retrieved from www.aspeninstitute.org/publications/putting-it-all-together/

Bishop, R. S. (1990). Mirrors, windows, and sliding glass doors. *Perspectives: Choosing and Using Books for the Classroom, 6*(3), ix–xi.

Cartaya, P. (2017). *The epic fail of Arturo Zamora*. New York, NY: Puffin Books.

Dolghan, J., Kelly, K., & Zelkha, S. (2010). *Authentic assessments for the English classroom*. Urbana, IL: National Council of Teachers of English.

Duncan-Andrade, J., & Morrell, E. (2005). Turn up that radio, teacher: Popular cultural pedagogy in new century urban schools. *Journal of School Leadership, 15*(3), 284–304.

Educating all Learners. (2020). Retrieved from https://educatingalllearners.org/

Fletcher, R., & Portalupi, J. (2001). *Writing workshop: The essential guide*. Portsmouth, NH: Heinemann.

Gallup, Inc. (2014). *State of America's schools report*. Retrieved from www.gallup.com/education/269648/state-america-schools-report.aspx

Gay, G. (2002). *Culturally responsive teaching: Theory, research and practice*. New York, NY: Teacher's College Press.

Grisham, D. L., & Wolsey, T. D. (2006). Recentering the middle school classroom as a vibrant learning community: Students, literacy, and technology intersect. *Journal of Adolescent & Adult Literacy, 49*(8), 648–660.

Hurst, B., Wallace, R., & Nixon, S. B. (2013). The impact of social interaction on student learning. *Reading Horizons: A Journal of Literacy and Language Arts, 52*(4), 375–398.

International Literacy Association. (2017). *Literacy assessment: What everyone needs to know*. Retrieved from www.literacyworldwide.org/docs/default-source/where-we-stand/literacy-assessment-brief.pdf?sfvrsn=efd4a68e_4

Jones, L. M., & Mitchell, K. J. (2016). Defining and measuring youth digital citizenship. *New Media & Society, 18*(9), 2063–2079.

Juliani, A. J. (2015). *Inquiry and innovation in the classroom: Using 20% time, genius hour, and PBL to drive student success*. New York, NY: Routledge.

Krebs, D., & Zvi, G. (2015). *The genius hour guidebook: Fostering passion, wonder, and inquiry in the classroom*. New York, NY: Routledge.

Kyei-Blankson, L., Ntuli, E., & Donnelly, H. (2019). Establishing the importance of interaction and presence to student learning in online environments. *Journal of Interactive Learning Research, 30*(4), 539–560.

Ladson-Billings, G. (1995). But that's just good teaching! The case for culturally relevant pedagogy. *Theory into Practice, 34*(3), 159–165.

Lyiscott, J. (2019). *Black appetite. White food.* New York, NY: Routledge Eye on Education.

Machado, E. (2017). Culturally sustaining pedagogy in the literacy classroom. *Literacy Now.* Retrieved from www.literacyworldwide.org/blog/literacy-now/2017/05/31/culturally-sustaining-pedagogy-in-the-literacy-classroom

McTighe, J., & Wiggins, G. (2013). *Essential questions: Opening doors to student understanding.* Alexandria, VA: ASCD.

Milner, J. O., Milner, L. M., & Mitchell, J. F. (2012). *Bridging English* (5th ed.). Boston, MA: Pearson.

Myroup, S. (2020.) Writing conferences for effective instruction. *Virginia English Journal, 70*(1). Retrieved from https://digitalcommons.bridgewater.edu/vej/vol70/iss1/8/#

National Council of Teachers of English. (2016). *Professional knowledge for the teaching of writing.* Retrieved from https://ncte.org/statement/teaching-writing/

National Council of Teachers of English. (2018). *Literacy assessment: Definitions, principles, and practices.* Retrieved from https://ncte.org/statement/assessmentframingst/

National Council of Teachers of English. (2020). *Expanding formative assessment for equity and agency.* Retrieved from https://ncte.org/statement/expanding-formative-assessment/

National Council of Teachers of English & International Reading Association. (1996). *NCTE/IRA standards for the English language arts.* Retrieved from https://ncte.org/resources/standards/ncte-ira-standards-for-the-english-language-arts/

National Writing Project & Nagin, C. (2006). *Because writing matters: Improving student writing in our schools.* San Francisco, CA: Jossey-Bass.

Nierenberg, A. (2020). Students, parents and teachers tell their stories of remote learning. *The New York Times.* Retrieved from www.nytimes.com/2020/10/14/education/learning/students-parents-teachers-remote-stories.html

Paris, D. (2012). Culturally sustaining pedagogy: A needed change in stance, terminology, and practice. *Educational Researcher, 41*(3), 93–97.

Pasternak, D. L (2007). Is technology used as practice? A survey analysis of preservice English teachers' perceptions and classroom practices. *Contemporary Issues in Technology and Teacher Education, 7*(3), 140–157.

Quin, D. (2016). Longitudinal and contextual associations between teacher–student relationships and student engagement: A systematic review. *Review of Educational Research, 87*(2), 345–387.

Rhine, S., & Bailey, M. (2011). Enhancing in-class participation in a Web 2.0 world. In C. Wankel (Ed.), *Educating educators with social media (cutting-edge technologies in higher education)* (Vol. 1, pp. 303–325). Bingley: Emerald Group Publishing Limited.

Richards, G. (2000). Why use computer technology? *English Journal, 90*(2), 38–41.

Richards, J. (2012). Teacher stress and coping strategies: A national snapshot. *Educational Forum, 76*, 299–316.

Rosenblatt, L. (1968). *Literature as exploration.* New York, NY: Noble and Noble.

Ruday, S. (2016). *The multimedia writing toolkit: Helping students incorporate graphics and videos for authentic purposes, grades 3–8.* New York, NY: Routledge Eye on Education.

Ruday, S. (2018). *The first-year English teacher's guidebook: Strategies for success.* New York, NY: Routledge Eye on Education.

Ruday, S., & Caprino, K. (2021). *Inquiry-based literature instruction in the 6–12 classroom: A hands-on guide for deeper learning.* New York, NY: Routledge Eye on Education.

Samuels, C. A. (2020). Closing COVID-19 equity gaps in schools. *Education Week.* Retrieved from www.edweek.org/leadership/closing-covid-19-equity-gaps-in-schools/2020/09

Singer, N. (2020). Teaching in the pandemic: "This is not sustainable". *The New York Times.* Retrieved from www.nytimes.com/2020/11/30/us/teachers-remote-learning-burnout.html

Swenson, J., Rozema, R., Young, C. A, McGrail, E., & Whitin, P. (2005). Beliefs about technology and the preparation of English teachers: Beginning the conversation. *Contemporary Issues in Technology and Teacher Education, 5*(3/4), 210–236.

Van Sluys, K. (2011). *Becoming writers in the elementary classroom.* Urbana, IL: NCTE.

Wiggins, G. (1998). *Education assessment: Designing assessments to inform and improve student performance.* San Francisco, CA: Jossey-Bass.

Wiggins, G., & McTighe, J. (2005). *Understanding by design.* Upper Saddle River, NJ: Pearson.

Young, C. A., & Bush, J. (2004). Teaching the English language arts with technology: A critical approach and pedagogical framework. *Contemporary Issues in Technology and Teacher Education, 4*(1), 1–22.

V
Appendices

Appendix A

Forms, Templates, and Graphic Organizers

This Appendix contains resources designed to help you put the ideas discussed in this book into action in your own remote English language arts instruction. The forms, templates, and graphic organizers provided here will guide your instructional practice and help you engage your students in effective remote English language arts learning.

Text You Used	Example of the Focal Strategy or Concept in the Text	Why You Feel the Strategy or Concept Is Important to the Effectiveness of the Text

Figure 3.1 Graphic Organizer for Published Text Analysis

Title and Brief Description of the Student's Piece	A Specific Strength of the Piece You Identified	A Concrete Suggestion for Improvement You Shared With the Student

Figure 3.2 Writing Conference Graphic Organizer

Student's name:

Date:

The day's focal strategy:

The Text You're Teaching	A Key Issue in the Text	Why Understanding This Issue Will Benefit Students	Some Activities You'll Use to Help Students Engage With This Issue

Figure 4.1 Key Issues Planning Chart

Writing	Reading	Language study
• Strong verbs • Specific nouns • Connotation-rich words • Engaging leads • Sensory detail	• Inferences • Connections • Analysis of mood • Predictions • Context clues	• Domain-specific vocabulary relevant to students' authentic experiences • Examples of word roots students encounter in their out-of-school lives

Figure 5.1 Examples of Literacy Concepts and Strategies

Copyright material from Sean Ruday and Jennifer Cassidy (2022), *Remote Teaching and Learning in the Middle and High ELA Classroom*, Routledge

Assessment	Brief Description	Why It Aligns With Remote Teaching and Learning
Website on a social issue	Students can create websites on social issues reflected in texts they've read, using those texts as support.	This assessment format provides students with authentic opportunities for students to share their ideas in ways that are meant to be created remotely for remote audiences, creating a strong alignment with remote instruction.
Podcast on a social issue	Similar to the previously described websites, students can create podcasts on social issues in the texts they've read and use those texts to support their ideas.	Podcasts can make outstanding remote assessments because they are meant to be shared remotely and align with both individual and collaborative work. For example, students can create podcasts on their own, or they can interview others and remotely incorporate their perspectives.
Writing for real-world audiences	Students can write on issues that matter to them and share those perspectives in authentic ways, such as posting them on Google Docs and sharing those links on social media, writing letters to online newspapers and magazines, and writing blog posts and comments that are read by authentic audiences.	By writing for real-world audiences, students can see that writing is not something just done for school: it can be done to share ideas in authentic, real-world ways. Through doing this, students are able to gain practice and experience with writing concepts while also sharing their perspectives with others who go beyond their teacher and classmates.

Figure 7.1 Possible Authentic Summative Assessments

Copyright material from Sean Ruday and Jennifer Cassidy (2022), *Remote Teaching and Learning in the Middle and High ELA Classroom*, Routledge

Assessment	Brief Description	Why It Aligns With Remote Teaching and Learning
Virtual panel conferences and webinars	In virtual panel conferences and webinars, students share ideas about key concepts they've studied and their unique perspectives on these ideas. Students present on concepts that are thematically aligned but offer their unique perspectives on these issues.	These panels and webinars provide excellent opportunities for remote learning evaluation because they create ways for students to express ideas and apply key understandings. This assessment format aligns well with culturally relevant and inquiry-based instruction because it provides excellent opportunities for students to provide their unique perspectives on conceptually aligned topics.
Infographics and one-pagers	Infographics and one-pagers are documents that use graphics and images to express key ideas about a character, text, theme, or concept. They allow students to combine words and images to effectively convey their ideas.	These documents, through their combination of visual features and student-created texts, purposefully incorporate digital tools in ways that call for students to express their knowledge. They are created and shared online in ways that align with features of remote learning and provide teachers with clear understandings of how well students have grasped key content.

Figure 7.1 (Continued)

Writing	Reading	Language Study

Copyright material from Sean Ruday and Jennifer Cassidy (2022), *Remote Teaching and Learning in the Middle and High ELA Classroom*, Routledge

Appendix B

A Guide for Book Studies

This book is well suited for groups of teachers using the text as a book study as they meet and discuss the successes and challenges they're experiencing in their English language arts instruction. If you're interested in discussing the ideas, information, and suggestions in this text with other teachers in order to learn with and from them, we recommend using this guide to facilitate your conversations. The guide provides key discussion questions to consider as you read and reflect on each of the book's chapters. These questions are designed to help you think about key issues in the text and to spark conversations with your colleagues about how you can apply the book's information to your own remote English language arts instruction.

Discussion Questions—Introduction

- Early in this introductory chapter, we list a number of questions that we (Sean and Jennifer) have asked ourselves about remote English language arts instruction. Select one of those questions that stands out to you as important and relevant. Why does this question resonate with you?
- This chapter discusses the information and topics we explore in this book. What is a topic you're especially interested to explore?

Copyright material from Sean Ruday and Jennifer Cassidy (2022), *Remote Teaching and Learning in the Middle and High ELA Classroom*, Routledge

Discussion Questions—Chapter 1: Building a Learning Community in the Time of Remote Instruction

- What are some ways you have built strong learning communities in your face-to-face classes? Reflect on some key features of those communities. While the methods of engagement will certainly be different, what are some ways you believe you could build similarly strong communities in your remote instruction?
- In this chapter, we provide four recommendations:
    - Conduct informal check-ins about noncurricular topics.
    - Share your own excitement, vulnerability, and personality.
    - Model what curiosity and learning look like for you.
    - Center students' identities and experiences in the curriculum.

What is a way you have done or will do one of these things in your remote instruction?

Discussion Questions—Chapter 2: Class Discussion and Student Collaboration in a New Era

- Based on the ideas and information in this chapter, what are some methods and tools you'll use to engage your students in remote class discussion and in collaborative activities?
- In this chapter's recommendations section, we describe a variety of suggestions for maximizing the effectiveness of class discussions. What are some practices you'll incorporate to make your students' class discussions and collaborations as effective as possible?

Discussion Questions—Chapter 3: A New Format of Writing and Grammar Instruction

- Based on your reading of this chapter and your experiences, what do you believe are some especially important aspects of effective writing and grammar instruction?
- In this chapter, we explain that "[w]hile the specific methods of delivery and collaboration will certainly differ, we feel that all these components of effective writing instruction can be achieved

in remote learning." With this in mind, which remote learning tools and features will you use as you support your students' understanding of writing strategies and grammatical concepts?

Discussion Questions—Chapter 4: Literature Instruction in the Remote Environment

- In this chapter, we discuss the ideas of enter, explore, and extend (Milner et al., 2012) and their importance to effective literature instruction. Now that you've explored these concepts and the remote learning information discussed in the chapter, reflect on how you would put each of these components of literature instruction into action in your own remote English language arts instruction. Some questions that can help you reflect on this topic are as follows:
  - What are some specific practices and tools you would implement? Why do you think those practices and tools will benefit your students?
  - What are some remote learning resources you would use to support your students as they engage with literary works remotely? Why do you feel these resources would be effective ways to support students?

Discussion Questions—Chapter 5: Culturally Relevant and Sustaining Teaching and Learning in Remote Contexts

- In this chapter, we explain that "[a]s Ladson-Billings (1995) and Paris (2012) describe, culturally relevant and culturally sustaining pedagogy is essential to creating equitable learning experiences for students" and "is characterized by instructional practices that value and center students' identities, which helps create opportunities for students' academic success." How have you centered students' identities in your English language arts instruction? How do you feel doing so contributed to equitable learning experiences for your students?
- What are some ways you will use the tools and features of remote learning as you incorporate culturally relevant and sustaining pedagogy in your instruction?

Discussion Questions—Chapter 6: The Role of Inquiry in Remote Teaching and Learning

- Reflect on the features of essential questions (McTighe & Wiggins, 2013) and the attributes of inquiry-based English language arts instruction (Ruday & Caprino, 2021) discussed in this chapter. Based on this information and the other ideas discussed in the chapter, why do you think inquiry-based English language arts instruction can create strong learning experiences for students?
- How will you use the attributes of remote instruction to create inquiry-based experiences for your students?

Discussion Questions—Chapter 7: Assessing Student Learning

- In this chapter, we discuss the importance of purposeful formative and summative assessments in English language arts instruction. What are some formative and summative assessments that have worked well for you in your instruction? What do you think made them effective?
- We also describe in this chapter a range of tactics teachers can incorporate when remotely implementing formative and summative assessments. What are some ways you will remotely assess student learning in your instruction?

Discussion Questions—Chapter 8: Strategies for Communication With Students and Caregivers

- What are some ways that communication with students and caregivers has changed for you during remote instruction?
- In this chapter, we provide four recommendations for communicating with students and caregivers:
  - Create an online class page that houses important information designed to help students succeed.
  - Share weekly agendas that describe what students will learn.
  - Provide caregivers with regular newsletters that communicate important information.
  - Hold remote conversations with caregivers that illustrate what students learn.

Copyright material from Sean Ruday and Jennifer Cassidy (2022), *Remote Teaching and Learning in the Middle and High ELA Classroom*, Routledge

Select one of these recommendations that especially stands out to you and reflect on how you'll put it into practice in your instruction.

Discussion Questions—Chapter 9: Reflecting on Technology

- One of the key concepts discussed in this chapter is the strategic use of technology. As we explain in the chapter, "[w]hile many technological tools and ideas can be beneficial for effective teaching and learning, we recommend starting your technology-based decision-making process by reflecting on your instructional goals and students, not specific innovations." What are some ways you can apply the concept of strategic technology use to your remote English language arts instruction?
- In this chapter, we also discuss the importance of equity-related issues in instructional technology, explaining that "[i]n order for us to create effective remote English language arts contexts designed to help facilitate student success, we need to reflect on ways to make our instructional technology equitable regarding a number of important issues, such as students' technological access, experience levels, and individual needs." What are some ways you will promote equity in your instructional technology use?

Discussion Questions—Chapter 10: Taking Care of Yourself

- What are some self-care activities that help you feel energized and centered in stressful times?
- In this chapter, we provide five recommendations for taking care of yourself during the stresses of remote instruction:
    - Don't wait to engage in self-care activities.
    - Schedule times to disconnect.
    - Create time to share and vent about your experiences.
    - Create times to socialize about anything but teaching.
    - Get lost in a passion.

- Select one of these recommendations and reflect on how you might put it into action.

Discussion Questions—Chapter 11: Key Takeaway Ideas

- ◆ In this chapter, we describe five key takeaway ideas to reflect on as you put the insights and examples described in this book into action in your classroom:
    - Reflect on and purposefully select technological tools.
    - Prioritize community-building in remote instruction.
    - Emphasize collaboration and interaction.
    - Center students' ideas and experiences.
    - Be purposeful about communication and self-care.

We invite you to select one of those recommendations that especially stands out to you and reflect on how you'll incorporate it in your remote English language arts instruction.

For Product Safety Concerns and Information please contact our EU representative GPSR@taylorandfrancis.com
Taylor & Francis Verlag GmbH, Kaufingerstraße 24, 80331 München, Germany

www.ingramcontent.com/pod-product-compliance
Lightning Source LLC
Chambersburg PA
CBHW080939300426
44115CB00017B/2883